O'BRIEN POCKET HISTORY OF
THE IRA

A concise yet comprehensive history of the IRA, from its inception in 1916 through the Good Friday Agreement of 1998 to the ensuing power struggles over armed force in the new millennium.

Born out of the struggle for independence from British colonial rule, the IRA is a movement with a long and complex history, linked back to the IRB. Intimately intertwined with the political party Sinn Féin, the Irish Republican Army was envisaged as the army of a new Irish Republic, an army for a future of peace and prosperity. In the late twentieth century that vision was corroded by a variety of factors – economic and political – and for many observers the IRA assumed a new, violent identity. This is the story of the IRA's long war and the evolution of the movement over the past eight decades.

BRENDAN O'BRIEN has reported on Northern Ireland as RTÉ's senior current affairs reporter since 1974, and has made three major documentaries about the IRA. He has won many awards for investigative journalism, including European Journalist of the Year 1998 and the Amnesty International Award 2001.

By the same author

The Long War: The IRA and Sinn Féin

Picture credits
The publisher and author wish to acknowledge the following for kind permission to reproduce photographs: **Picture section:** courtesy of John Osmond, pp. 1–2 (top and bottom); courtesy of Independent Newspapers, p. 3 (top), p.4 (top); courtesy of Senator Dan Neville, p. 3 (bottom), p.4 (bottom); courtesy of *An Phoblacht*, p.5 (top); courtesy of *The Irish Times*, p. 5 (bottom), p.6 (bottom); courtesy of Pacemaker Press International, p. 6 (top), p.8 (bottom); courtesy of the Press Association, p.7 (bottom). **Back cover:** image of Ruairí Ó Brádaigh courtesy of *The Irish Times*, image of Republican prisoners courtesy of John Osmund; **Front cover:** image courtesy of Derek Spiers/Report.

O'BRIEN POCKET HISTORY OF

The IRA

FROM 1916 ONWARDS

Brendan O'Brien

THE O'BRIEN PRESS
DUBLIN

This revised edition first published 2007
by The O'Brien Press Ltd,
12 Terenure Road East, Rathgar, Dublin 6, Ireland.
Tel: +353 1 4923333; Fax: +353 1 4922777
E-mail: books@obrien.ie
Website: www.obrien.ie
First published 1997
Reprinted 1997, 2000, 2001
Revised 2003, 2005, 2007.

ISBN: 978-1-84717-080-4

British Library Cataloguing-in-Publication Data
A catalogue reference for this title is available from the British Library

7 8 9 10 11 12
07 08 09 10

Typesetting, editing, layout, design: The O'Brien Press Ltd
Printing: Cox & Wyman Ltd

Contents

CREATING THE DREAM, 1916

The original leaders of the Irish Republican Army would be astonished to find now, more than eighty years later, there is still no thirty-two county Irish Republic. The received wisdom of the 1920s was that the new artificial construction, the Border dividing Ireland into the six-county Northern Ireland province of the UK and the twenty-six county Irish Free State, would wither with time. With it would wither Britain's last vestiges of power in Ireland. Yet the unthinkable *was* happening. Crossing a new millennium another generation of IRA activists was fighting the same fight. The Partition of Ireland and British jurisdiction over Northern Ireland had become more, not less, embedded over the years and gained more, not less, enduring nationalist acquiescence. Looking beyond the 2000s an independent unitary Irish state, ruled from Dublin, was widely regarded as a remote and impossible dream. For a great many would-be Irish republicans, even the dreaming had stopped.

Yes, the Good Friday Agreement of 1998 re-kindled hope. But Óglaigh na hÉireann had been forced to accept unthinkable compromise, despite being more entrenched than at any stage since the 1920s. The modern IRA, reconstituted in December 1969 and on the offensive for most of the time since August 1971, had sustained the longest-ever unbroken armed resistance against British rule in Ireland. Yet they had not achieved their goal. When the Army Council confidently declared a unilateral cessation of military operations in August 1994 to enter round-table negotiations, they received no guarantee of winning the Republic. They had neither been victorious nor had they been defeated. Not to be defeated by overwhelming

British forces during almost a quarter of a century of armed action was in itself regarded as a major success. But with no victory in sight ambitions had become chastened. The unambiguous demand for a British withdrawal from Ireland had been replaced by the language of compromise. And the fact that the IRA had effectively come to recognise the legitimacy of the southern state, for so long regarded as an illegal puppet regime, was a very real manifestation of their failure.

When the IRA's cessation of violence broke down in early 1996 most of the volunteers and local commanders were happy to be back in action, back at the British, ready as always to finish the business. One more push and the British would be forced to 'face their responsibilities', as it was now ambiguously put in Army Council statements. The resumption of armed struggle, however, reopened old divisions over politics and armed force; divisions which had bedevilled modern Irish separatists ever since Pádraig Pearse publicly proclaimed the still-elusive thirty-two county Irish Republic around noon on Easter Monday, 24 April 1916. That was, in effect, the time and date when the Irish Republican Army was born.

THE EASTER RISING

The 1916 Easter Rising in Dublin, as begun by Pearse's proclamation, was not a neat and tidy affair between a newly formed Republican Army and the British forces. In the first instance, it was not so much a rising, more an attempted military coup, secretly plotted by a handful of mainly unknown men. The self-proclaimed Army of the Republic was at first an uncertain collection of dedicated militarists; primarily Irish Volunteers supported by the Irish Citizen Army and even smaller groups like the Hibernian

Rifles, all under the command of the Military Council of the Irish Republican Brotherhood.

This was no cohesive fighting force welded together over time with a disciplined structure and ideology. Some were separatists but not republicans. The Irish Volunteers, founded in 1913, was a broad church numbering close to 200,000, few of whom were armed and most of whom in 1914 followed the lead of John Redmond, moderate leader of the Irish Parliamentary Party, in pledging Ireland's support for Britain in the Great War against Germany. Those Volunteers who dissented from Redmond's call numbered just over a thousand under Chief of Staff Eoin MacNeill. And even when the Rising came in 1916 it was started against the wishes of MacNeill, who correctly argued that it would end in military disaster and public hostility.

Ideologically, the small Irish Citizen Army, formed by the revolutionary socialist trade union leader James Connolly, was a group apart. Connolly had far more radical ambitions than people like Pádraig Pearse and the traditionalist Roman Catholic Hibernian Rifles group, connected with the Ancient Order of Hibernians. Alongside this collection of disparate organisations was a new political grouping called Sinn Féin, meaning 'Ourselves Alone'. At the time Sinn Féin was more separatist than the Irish Parliamentary Party but, in proposing a dual monarchy for Britain and Ireland, was not republican.

Where there was cohesion was within the Irish Republican Brotherhood (IRB), the main driving force behind the attempted military coup. The IRB was a dedicated, secretive body formed in March 1858, first called the Irish Revolutionary Brotherhood, avowedly republican and militaristic with support among the immigrant Irish in the emergent United States, where it was known as Clann na Gael.

Despite these uncomfortable combinations, a single military group *had* come together, acting within the terms of the decision adopted on 9 September 1914, by the Irish Republican Brotherhood, to strike against Britain at some time during the war which had just begun. When it came to it, the bulk of Irish separatists were unwilling to take up arms against what was then their own legal government at a time of war. Many had enlisted and were dug into trenches in foreign fields, fighting Britain's fight. In addition, the Liberal government in London had developed a policy of Home Rule for Ireland. The fuse of armed resistance to British policy came not from republicans demanding more but from the Ulster Volunteers demanding less. Formed in 1912 these Unionists were pledged in blood to fight against Home Rule, a pledge backed in part by elements in the British Conservative Party and in the British Army. Still, some measure of independence for Ireland, albeit under the Crown, was a probability at war's end. Given the electoral strength of Redmond's Irish Party, the advocates of Home Rule, it seemed a majority of Irish people would have been content with that.

It was virtually unimaginable that the 1916 Proclamation declaring Ireland a republic, read on that ordinary Easter Monday to a bemused and disinterested Dublin population outside the General Post Office, would in time become the bedrock of 20th century Irish republican ideology. Headed 'POBLACHT na HÉIREANN: THE PROVISIONAL GOVERNMENT OF THE IRISH REPUBLIC TO THE PEOPLE OF IRELAND', it read:

> Irishmen and Irishwomen: in the name of God and of the dead generations from which she receives her old tradition of manhood, Ireland, through us, summons her children to her flag and strikes for her freedom.

Having organised and trained her manhood through her secret revolutionary organisation, the Irish Republican Brotherhood, and through her open military organisation, the Irish Volunteers and the Irish Citizen Army, having patiently perfected her discipline, having resolutely waited for the right moment to reveal itself, she now seizes that moment and, supported by her exiled children in America and by gallant allies in Europe, but relying in the first on her own strength, she strikes in full confidence of victory.

We declare the right of the Irish people to the ownership of Ireland and to the unfettered control of Irish destinies to be sovereign and indefeasible. The long usurpation of that right by a foreign people and government has not extinguished that right nor can it ever be extinguished except by the destruction of the Irish people. In every generation the Irish people have asserted their right to national freedom and sovereignty: six times during the past three hundred years they have asserted it in arms. Standing on that fundamental right and again asserting it in arms in the face of the world, we hereby declare the Irish Republic as a Sovereign Independent State; and we pledge our lives and the lives of our comrades-in-arms to the cause of its freedom, of its welfare and of its exhaltation among the nations.

The Irish Republic is entitled to, and hereby claims, the allegiance of every Irishman and Irishwoman. The Republic guarantees religious and civil liberty, equal rights and equal opportunities to all its citizens, and declares its resolve to pursue the happiness and prosperity of the whole nation and of all its parts, cherishing all the children of the nation equally, and oblivious of the differences carefully fostered by an alien government, which have divided a minority from the majority in the past.

Until our arms have brought the opportune moment for the establishment of a permanent National Government, representative of the whole people of Ireland and elected by the suffrages of all her men and women, the Provisional Government, hereby constituted, will administer the civil and military affairs of the Republic in trust for the people.

We place the cause of the Irish Republic under the protection of the Most High God, Whose blessing we invoke upon our arms, and we pray that no one who serves that cause will dishonour it by cowardice, inhumanity or rapine. In this supreme hour, the Irish nation must, by its valour and discipline and by the readiness of its children to sacrifice themselves for the common good, prove itself worthy of the august destiny to which it is called.

Signed on behalf of the Provisional Government: Thomas J Clarke, Seán Mac Diarmada, Thomas MacDonagh, PH Pearse, Eamonn Ceannt, James Connolly, Joseph Plunkett.

It seemed a preposterous and outrageous statement: these seven men claiming to be the Provisional government of a new Irish Republic, attempting to overthrow the might of the British Empire in an open battle. In any event, by the time the Proclamation was read out the seven signatories knew that defeat was inevitable. They would not have the arms to do the job as planned. A German arms ship, the *Aud* destined for the insurgents, was intercepted by the British off the southwest coast days before the Rising. This led Eoin MacNeill, a reluctant and late supporter of the secret plot, to send orders for the operation to be called off. Those who proceeded, particularly Pearse, were engaged in a blood sacrifice, intent on adding another glorious chapter to the story enshrined in the Proclamation, passing on the flame to another generation. As for leadership, Pádraig Pearse was more a political romantic than a military strategist.

Still, the insurgents put up a real fight, though the action was confined to Dublin. Only tiny and sporadic support came from the country. Using vastly superior military might the British forces crushed the insurrection to unconditional surrender at 3.30pm on Saturday 29 April. One of the last groups to hold out was the company of Irish Volunteers at Bolands Bakery on the outskirts of the city under the command of Eamon de Valera.

When it was over, much of central Dublin lay in ruins and many of the city's working-class slum areas were damaged by stray over-fire. The people were not amused by the antics of the insurgents, their seemingly farcical Proclamation and their extraordinary claim to be the provisional government of the country. Political and press reaction was hostile in the extreme.

In that atmosphere the British government, with a real war on its hands to the east and not wanting a weakened western flank, decided on the toughest of reprisal measures. Under the new command of General Sir John Maxwell, the government's military response was to crush both the spirit and the flesh of this fledgling militant Irish republicanism. The leaders would be executed, hundreds of others would be given penal servitude, hard labour and deportation. Executions and deportations had proven effective in quelling past Irish military adventures: 1798 – Theobald Wolfe Tone; 1803 – Robert Emmet; 1848 – Young Irelanders; 1867 – Fenians. Then, the rebels and their cause had failed to stir the broad public conscience and life carried on as normal. It would be the same this time.

But far from repeating itself, history took a dramatic turn. This time, Britain's crushing and ruthless measures failed even on their most justifiable military level, that of keeping her western flank quiet in time of war. Irish nationalism was stirred like never before. From 3 May 1916, fifteen leaders were executed, including all seven signatories to the Proclamation. A severely wounded James Connolly was shot by firing squad while tied to a chair. De Valera's life was spared on the grounds that he was a foreign, American, citizen. In terms of the effect on militant Irish republicanism, the British miscalculation was immense. It proved the catalyst for the merging of the disparate fighting forces into a broadly supported Irish Republican Army allied to a new political force in the land, Sinn Féin.

FIGHTING FOR THE REPUBLIC, 1916–1921

The reorganisation of militant Irish separatism was not automatic. Nor did it follow immediately on the heels of the 1916 executions and imprisonments. The centre had been taken away and time was needed. But in historical terms the re-grouping was exceptionally swift, as though by-passing the gap of a generation. Within two years the obscure new organisation called Sinn Féin, with its strange theories about national self-reliance and headed by its aloof new President, Eamon de Valera, had swept aside the long-established Irish Party in a tidal wave of electoral support for a defiant separatist parliament (Dáil Éireann) in Dublin.

The Irish Volunteers had been skilfully re-shaped into a people's fighting force with a popular mandate, emerging as the Irish Republican Army, the army of the Republic as declared by Dáil Éireann. The principal architect of that military re-shaping was the dynamic and enigmatic Michael Collins. This new chapter began on 25 October 1917, with a Sinn Féin Árd Fheis (annual conference) combined with an undercover Army Convention. At those meetings Sinn Féin ditched its dual monarchy policy and the Irish Republican Army (still called the Irish Volunteers) began taking a unified shape with a new command structure under Chief-of-Staff, Cathal Brugha, and his deputy, Richard Mulcahy, with Collins as Director of Organisation.

In this valley period between 1916 and 1918 the forging of unity among Irish separatists ebbed and flowed. Sinn Féin won and lost a series of by-elections. The party ran on a policy of abstention, that is, not taking their seats in the Westminster Parliament if elected. This policy was in large part designed to act as a substitute for armed action. The majority of Irish people was still more willing to support political struggle than military rebellion.

But the British government again assisted the militarists. In early 1917 the new British Prime Minister, David Lloyd George, enraged moderate Ireland by seeming to make the prospect of post-war Home Rule for Ireland conditional on the introduction of conscription in Ireland during the war. Conscription was *the* major emotive point of departure for most Irish people. Volunteering to fight for Britain was one thing. Being conscripted into the British Army was quite another. Linking conscription to Home Rule was intolerable. Lloyd George's manoeuvres resulted in massive anti-British disaffection and waves of recruits for Michael Collins. It was a high price paid by the Liberal government, normally a friend of Irish Home Rule, since World War I ended in November 1918 with America's vital assistance to Britain and without the need for conscription in Ireland.

FINDING A ROLE

All this time the IRA were re-organising but not fighting. Support at street level and on the crossroads was high, in sentiment at least. There was still no certainty of another round against the British. Quite the opposite. Sinn Féin was sweeping up the sentiment and the physical force men were in the background, biding their time.

The general election of December 1918 appeared to justify Sinn Féin's preference for political abstention rather than military rebellion. They had a prodigious victory. Out of 105 Irish seats, Sinn Féin on a republican ticket won 73, the Irish Parliamentary Party still advocating Home Rule under the Crown, 6. It was a stunning turnaround though the 'first past the post' electoral system masked the fact that, where voters had a choice, about a third of the nationalist or separatist electorate had voted for the old Irish Parliamentary Party. (The votes cast were: Sinn Féin 485,105; Irish Parliamentary Party 237,393. No votes were counted in twenty-four constituencies where Sinn Féin candidates were returned unopposed.) The Unionists, mostly in the northern province of Ulster, having resisted Home Rule by threat of force, won 26 seats with 315,394 votes, further copper-fastening the emerging divide on the island. Furthermore, although the voting system had given Sinn Féin a landslide of seats, they had won a minority of votes cast on the island as a whole. It was a good deal less than a mandate for an unfettered all-Ireland republic. But history had been made. A page had turned in Ireland's fortunes. Written on it were portents of further grief and division.

For a start the Unionists and Irish Party members took their seats at Westminster. Sinn Féiners stayed at home as they had pledged. Most of the successful Sinn Féin candidates were in prison or on the run. But those who could met as a body in Dublin on 21 January 1919 formed a defiant Dáil Éireann and voted a Declaration of Independence, based on the Proclamation of the Republic of Easter Monday 1916. This had the effect of legitimising the Rising and the Republic. (It also further links the lifespan of the IRA or 'Army of the Republic' back to 1916.) Members of this first Dáil Éireann took the following oath:

> I ... do solemnly swear (or affirm) that I do not and shall not yield a voluntary support to any pretended government authority or power within Ireland hostile and inimical thereto, and I do swear (or affirm) that, to the best of my knowledge and ability, I will support and defend the Irish Republic and the Government of the Irish Republic, which is Dáil Éireann, against all enemies, foreign and domestic, and I will bear true faith and allegiance to the same, and that I take this obligation freely, without any mental reservation or purpose of evasion, so help me God.

It was after the 1919 Dáil declared Ireland a Republic that the Irish Volunteers called themselves Óglaigh na hÉireann (Irish Republican Army). Yet at that stage the Dáil did not control the IRA. A battle was on for hearts and minds over whether to resort again to force. Sinn Féin had received a massive mandate on a pledge to win independence through passive resistance. At the same time IRA leaders like Mulcahy, Brugha and Collins were also Sinn Féin leaders (de Valera was president of both organisations) and the secretive Irish Republican Brotherhood continued to exist, with a further overlap of membership. The lines between militarism and politics were even more blurred by the fact that a number of de Valera's eight-man 'Cabinet' were IRA leaders, including Michael Collins who had been appointed Minister for Finance. Collins was pivotally placed in both camps and could push for physical force from within and without. The man he most needed to persuade was Arthur Griffith, chief advocate of the passive resistance policy, founder of Sinn Féin and now Chairman of the rebel Dáil Éireann and Minister for Home Affairs. Griffith was a formidable opponent of the early use of force.

In reality, then, the pre-eminence of the IRA in the struggle for independence came about by provocative actions of the militarists attempting to force the pace combined with ambiguity in the ranks of Sinn Féin and the violent responses of Crown Forces on the ground. The first salvo had been fired on the day Dáil Éireann was convened, 21 January 1919. At Soloheadbeg, Co Tipperary, a maverick action by a group led by Seán Treacy left two policemen dead in a surprise ambush, tripping an undeclared 'War of Independence'. It wasn't until April 1921, after more than two years of escalating guerrilla warfare, that Dáil Éireannn accepted responsibility for IRA actions. By then the militarists had finally won the day. The IRA emerged as a legitimised Army of the Republic, the cutting edge in the fight for recognition of the Republic by the British government. That period, 1919 to 1921, was the high-point in the IRA's existence. In the end, however, they failed to win British recognition and failed to hold the Republic.

Much later events would see the IRA Army Council take to themselves the powers of the Provisional government of the 1919 Republic and Dáil, even as their strength and influence almost died and another type of Irish state took root. To the IRA and Sinn Féin, that 1919 Republic and Dáil, based on a thirty-two county mandate, remained the only true Republic and Dáil, all later 'Partitionist' institutions being treasonable. For more than eighty years afterwards, through splits and splinters, the IRA agitated and fought to win back the all-Ireland Republic as proclaimed in 1916, 'legitimised' in 1919 and to which they had taken an oath of allegiance. That was what kept them in existence. The fact that the Unionists in the north received a different mandate entirely was of no consequence to the IRA: the Irish people as a whole had spoken, albeit using the quirks of the British electoral system.

COLLINS'S FLYING COLUMNS

All of that was for an uncertain future. For the present, in 1919, the emergent IRA was growing in audacity and confidence. But the re-shaping of the Volunteers into a hit-and-run guerrilla army was not the result of a grand design. It grew by bits and pieces and often with events dictating Collins's thinking. One simple lesson was learned from 1916, however. This time they would not foolishly take on the might of the British in open battle. Theirs would be a war of surprise and stealth. Arms were at a premium. After Seán Treacy's unit's solo run at Soloheadbeg other units took courage in their hands and struck, raiding for arms in particular.

But a major objective of their actions was the intimidation of the Royal Irish Constabulary (RIC). Being a locally based police force, 9,000 of them spread around the country and living in the same towns and villages as the IRA activists, these men's local intelligence was vital to British military control. But, as locals, they were highly vulnerable to physical attack and to the charge of treachery against their own people. So an essential tactic was the intimidation of the RIC. (The tactic had been copied in large measure by the modern-day IRA). From May to December 1919 eighteen RIC men were killed. The tactic of intimidation extended to civilians working for or supplying goods to the police.

In addition, Collins was intent on infiltrating the core of British intelligence in Ireland, the G Division, the feared 'G-men' detectives of the Dublin Metropolitan Police. One night in April 1919, Collins himself was smuggled into the inner sanctum of Detective Headquarters, where he examined files, including his own, and pored over the RIC's entire countrywide intelligence network. This undiscovered secret adventure gave Collins the information he needed to take on the daunting task of undermining RIC operations. It made him a formidable adversary of the British. As the IRA's 'flying columns' stepped up their attacks, outlying RIC posts and barracks became untenable, forcing the police to retreat to larger more fortified compounds.

Parallel with this still to be 'legitimised' IRA guerrilla warfare, the rebel Dáil Éireann was setting about establishing a system of dual power structures: police, tax collecting, courts, local government bodies, all answerable to the self-proclaimed Republic's authority. This was Sinn Féin theory put into practice, the powerhouse theoretician being Sinn Féin's founder Arthur Griffith. Griffith's theory dictated that this dual power set-up would result in the British system of government dying as the parallel republican structure took root. The plan had considerable localised success, enough to make the British government take the rebel Irish parliament seriously. The essentials of British power, however, their centralised civil service and, ultimately the British Army, held firm.

Nonetheless, all of these combined events, including the smouldering Unionist edifice, forced the British Prime Minister, David Lloyd George, to accept a form of defeat which, in the final analysis, was to wreck forever the republicans' push for recognition of the all-Ireland republic. In December 1919 Lloyd George proposed a Bill to partition Ireland, granting Home Rule to two separate parts, 'Ulster' and the rest. The IRA's response to this pessimistic proposition was to escalate their guerrilla war. In turn the British government decided on a counter-policy of terror and oppression.

TERROR AND COUNTER-TERROR

By the spring of 1920 the RIC was a demoralised and depleted force. The British authorities set out to recruit sturdy volunteers in Britain itself with a view to enforcing the Crown's writ. When the first batch of recruits arrived they were immediately seen to be different from the regular police force. Their temporary uniforms, given to them in a state of urgency, were made of black leather and khaki. They had the look of paramilitary stormtroopers rather than police and were swiftly called the 'Black and Tans' by the rebel Irish. Even after the correct RIC uniforms were supplied, this title stuck in the mind and in the historic memory as a symbol of British oppression during this period, a period styled 'the Tan War'. The 'Black and Tans' were reinforced by a specialist quasipolice unit, the Auxiliary Cadets. That year, 1920 was the year the British government turned its full attention on Ireland, determined to rein in the rebels, north and south.

In the north the pattern, as always, was somewhat different. There, the majority Protestant and Unionist people felt they had a British birthright to defend and they began setting up local vigilante groups. The IRA had made little impact in northern Ulster until 1920. But when they did, the RIC adopted the same policy as further south. They retreated to more fortified central locations, abandoning small rural police stations. This left IRA 'flying columns' free to roam about, making ever more daring raids into Unionist enclaves.

The Protestants' response was to take the law into their own hands to defend their lands, their religion and their Britishness. As planters of the 17th century who were given Catholic lands their primary task as loyalists was always to defend the Protestant Crown against the Catholic enemy.

This they had done throughout the 17th and 18th centuries, until the Act of Union of 1800 bound Britain and Ireland together 'forever' and gave the loyalist Protestants the religious and economic protection they desired. From their perspective the republican/Catholic rebellion of the early 20th century was another in a long line of rebellions. Their 18th century history told them of Catholic 'Ribbon-men' waging guerrilla war against the Protestant 'Peep o'Day Boys'. This brand of Protestant regarded the IRA simply as disreputable thugs and vicious rebels, the 20th century variety of past villains. Viewed from the northern Protestant enclaves Britain's Dublin-based military and political regime was weak and vacillating. So defend themselves they would.

One of the most active organisers of Protestant vigilante units was Captain Sir Basil Brooke, a major landowner at Colebrooke in County Fermanagh and destined to be a future Prime Minister of Northern Ireland. Brooke had tried and failed to get the military authorities in Dublin to support his concept of an armed Special Constabulary. In reply, Protestants armed themselves, forming military-style units mostly under the command of former British Army officers. They made use of the pre-war illegally imported rifles of the Ulster Volunteer Force. The 20th century Irish battle-lines were being firmly fixed.

For the moment, in 1920, the IRA were focusing on defending the 'Republic' against escalating British measures of oppression. The British government sought a military victory over the rebels, particularly as other subject colonies of the British Empire were looking on with interest. Terror was met with terror. On 20 March, after the killing of an RIC man in the Cork area, Thomas MacCurtain, Lord Mayor of Cork and IRA Brigade Commander, was shot dead at his home in front of his wife. The deputy Lord Mayor Terence MacSwiney took over, and was later to make a major impact on the republican campaign.

As the battle-lines hardened, Collins ordered the executions of men accused as spies and informers. On Easter Sunday, 1920, in a major scorched earth-type offensive, IRA units destroyed by fire up to a hundred tax offices and more than three hundred abandoned RIC stations. In July 1920 came one of those events which sparked the smouldering hatreds of centuries past. On 17 July in Cork the IRA killed Colonel Smyth, the Divisional Commander of the RIC in Munster. As it happened, Col Smyth was a native of Banbridge, a largely Protestant town in the Planter county of Down in the northeast. Serious rioting erupted accross Co Down as reprisals against 'Sinn Féin property' and 'Sinn Féin workers' took place. Belfast ghettos became engulfed as did the massive shipyards, where an increasing number of Catholics had taken up jobs left vacant by Protestants who had gone and fought in the War.

The killing of Col Smyth and the rioting in Down was enough to set off one of Belfast's endemic sectarian conflicts. On 21 July Protestant shipyard workers decided to expel all Catholics from the yards, viciously attacking some and throwing others into the harbour. A three-day spree of street rioting and shooting in Belfast left eighteen people dead and 200 injured. It was one of those classic incidents where each side could justifiably accuse the other and which further entrenched loyalists and republicans in their ever-diverging political beliefs.

In the autumn of 1920 three events in swift succession sent Irish separatist emotions soaring to new heights. On 14 October Seán Treacy, the activist who had lit the fuse of the War of Independence, was shot dead in Dublin.

Meanwhile, Cork's new Lord Mayor Terence MacSwiney was on a much-publicised hunger strike along with nine other men who had been arrested for involvement in an IRA meeting in Cork City Hall. The men were demanding to be released and the British government, in the international spotlight, could not give way. One hunger-striker died on 17 October. But on 25 October, the most prestigious of the hunger-strikers, Lord Mayor MacSwiney died. Another man died a few hours later and the rest called off the protest. No more suffering was required.

MacSwiney's death made an enormous impact on Irish and British opinion. It also added considerable moral weight to the Irish separatist cause. This was immediately apparent when MacSwiney's body was moved from Brixton Prison for burial in Ireland. A mammoth procession through London saw the coffin escorted by illegal uniformed IRA volunteers and the entourage accompanied by fully robed priests and bishops.

Then, just six days later, on 1 November an eighteen-year-old IRA activist and medical student, Kevin Barry, was hanged for his part in an IRA operation in Dublin which left three policemen dead. Kevin Barry's young age had given his case another burst of public attention, including a highly charged campaign for the sentence to be commuted. Michael Collins had even contemplated a spectacular rescue mission, to blow open Mountjoy Prison in Dublin where Barry awaited his fate. The hanging of Kevin Barry took place in an atmosphere of near-hysterical religious fervour, including huge prayer vigils outside the prison walls. Coming so swiftly after Terence MacSwiney's hunger strike the cumulative emotive impact was great. Many moderate Irish hearts and minds were won over to the side of physical force.

In this atmosphere, and apparently with the wind at his back, Collins organised a high-risk and brutal military strike. On Sunday, 21 November 1920, in a concerted surprise operation, IRA units shot dead fourteen British secret service agents in their homes or lodgings, some in front of wives and family, and another five men, probably not agents at all. The agents worked directly to Col Ormonde Winter, head of British combined intelligence services in Ireland. Collins regarded them as deadly 'hit men', responsible for many undercover killing missions. It was a big blow to British intelligence and an audacious affront to British power in Ireland. The British responded in kind, though with recklessly little political finesse. They attacked civilians. The same day, a group of 'Black and Tans' fired into the crowd at Dublin's Croke Park during a Gaelic football match between Dublin and Tipperary. Fourteen people were killed and dozens injured.

Misguided and hamfisted as the Tans' action was, the Irish public knew it was a response to the morning's brutal doings by Collins's men. 'Bloody Sunday', as 21 November 1920 became known, could well have destroyed the IRA's new-found moral support-base and, for a time, Collins thought it had. Fear gripped the ordinary Irish, particularly in Dublin. Further reprisals were feared and rumoured. IRA activists and Sinn Féiners went into hiding. Within the British forces and political establishment there was a new determination to crush Collins's men. In the manner of things reactions and counter-reactions cancelled each other out and the IRA emerged with enhanced pride and public support.

Two events by year's end ensured that. First, pride: a week after 'Bloody Sunday', seventeen RIC Auxiliaries were killed in an IRA ambush at Kilmichael, Co Cork. It was the Auxiliaries' greatest single loss. Second, public support: on 11 December 1920 in a reprisal operation, units of the Auxiliaries set fire to whole sections of Cork City, including the City Hall, gutting many shops and civic buildings. Public outrage was further fuelled by British government denials that Crown Forces were involved.

By this stage it was clear that the IRA had the capacity and the support to take the fight to a conclusion. The conclusion would turn out to be far more difficult and complex than many single-minded volunteers in the 'flying columns' anticipated. Not too many IRA leaders showed signs of understanding the strength of northern Unionist resistance. The IRA's fight, as always, was with the British Crown Forces and, by the end of 1920, the IRA appeared to have them on the run. By then, the Irish cause was receiving considerable international attention. De Valera was in America drumming up support and cash. At home Arthur Griffith and Dáil Éireann had still not accepted political cover and responsibility for the IRA but the arguments against were wearing thin.

VICTORY IN SIGHT

As the fateful year of 1920 drew to a close the militarisation of the Irish problem was almost complete. The republicans' dual power structure, essentially a political apparatus, was crumbling, squeezed by the grip of British military might and the escalating IRA campaign. Politically too the self-proclaimed Irish Republic had failed to win recognition at the post-war Paris Peace Conference or, vitally, in the US, despite de Valera's best efforts. Dev returned to Ireland in December 1920 to a situation which relied almost entirely on the fighting capacity of the IRA to resist British pressure.

During the first part of 1921, as political feelers began to test the waters of compromise, murderous activities by both sides descended to even lower depths. The British burnt out Sinn Féin homes and hanged IRA activists. The IRA 'executed' up to seventy alleged spies and informers. On 25 May 1921 came one more determinant event. In another daring affront to British authority, the Dublin Brigade of the IRA captured the Custom House in Dublin and burnt it to a shell. Among the charred remains were the papers and records of nine administrative departments, including the vital one of tax-collecting, so essential to British government in Ireland. Six IRA men were killed and up to seventy captured as the British swooped. It was a costly loss to the IRA but, as the legends and ballads built up on the republican side, this was one of their best. The burning of the Custom House became a defining moment in the War of Independence. It was not so much a republican triumph as an event which caused both sides to pause.

Successful as they were in staying the pace, the IRA, perhaps about 200,000 strong, were a tired and under-armed force. Plans were in hand for a shipment from the US of new-style Thompson submachine guns, fifty of which arrived; but most were seized in New York in June. In addition, severe tensions were building up between Michael Collins and de Valera, who was re-asserting his control over events.

For their part the British were considering their options, the military men as before arguing that more troops would finish the job. They had thrown massive resources at the insurrection, including more than 50,000 troops, police, 'Tans', Auxiliaries and agents. Lloyd George could see its limitations. He inclined towards the politics of compromise, risking the wrath of powerful elements within the

British political and military establishments. After all, the 'Sinn Féiners' had begun as nothing more than a precocious band of treacherous rebels. In a sense both the British government and the IRA were torn between war or politics. A weary stalemate was setting in. Up to a point the IRA had achieved a victory. They had thwarted the British military offensive. The Republic was intact but only by dint of IRA resistance. It remained unrecognised by the British government and the Unionists and by a slumbering minority of Irish separatists. Internationally, only the new Soviet Russia gave it recognition. Yet they *had* forced Britain's hand. So too had the Unionists, bitter opponents of an Irish republic.

The general elections of 24 May 1921 were held under the terms of the 1920 Government of Ireland Act, setting up a northern (six county) and a southern (twenty-six county) parliament. This gave the Unionists a resounding victory in the new Northern Ireland, amidst claims of rampant gerrymandering. Sinn Féin copper-fastened their political hold over the 'Republic' by a quasi-democratic scheme of getting themselves elected unopposed to Dáil Éireann, which was still illegal and unrecognised by the British government. This meant that under the terms of the Government of Ireland Act 'Southern Ireland' opted out and the southern parliament lapsed. Events were underwriting the partition of Ireland. Endless strife was in prospect, even civil war.

A series of 'feelers', meetings and correspondence ensued, to determine if the basis for talks existed. On 25 June 1921 Eamon de Valera received a letter from the British Prime Minister, David Lloyd George, suggesting a peace conference. On 11 July the IRA agreed a truce. Óglaigh na hÉireann had reached its zenith. No other generation of militant Irish separatists had achieved this. Their rebellion against the Crown had not been snuffed out, as in the past and as Britain's generals had anticipated. Against all expectations they had kept faith with the men of 1916.

It was indeed an historical moment to savour. But what had the IRA achieved? Not the Republic. Though Michael Collins had engineered the war for that goal, Lloyd George had determined that the Republic would not be granted. In a series of subsequent written exchanges with de Valera the British Prime Minister made this plain. Lloyd George rejected de Valera's attempt to have the Irish delegation negotiate as representatives of an independent and sovereign state. In the end, de Valera accepted Lloyd George's terms of reference for the conference, set for London on 11 October 1921. Lloyd George had invited de Valera's delegation 'as spokesmen for the people whom you represent with a view to ascertaining how the association of Ireland with the community of nations known as the British Empire can best be reconciled with Irish national aspirations'.

This was a highly contentious form of words, seeming to cut out the prospect of an Irish Republic emerging from the negotiations. De Valera's acceptance of the invitation on this basis guaranteed compromise, not victory, for the republicans, given that the outcome would leave Ireland in 'association with ... the British Empire'. It seemed to herald an Ireland under the Crown in some form. In addition, in the run-up period, de Valera and the Dáil accepted that the northern Unionists could not be coerced by force into an Irish republic and, even, that each county could have the right to opt out. By that stage it was clear that the Unionists would not be part of an independent Irish state, even if one were to be negotiated.

To the die-hards in the IRA this unfortunate set of circumstances meant that war against the British would inevitably have to be resumed. But all relevant parties – de Valera, Collins and the 'Cabinet' in Dublin – acceded to the terms for talks. The dragon's teeth were sown, not for another round against the British or the Unionists but for a bloody civil war. Having reached its zenith in 1921, the Irish Republican Army was about to begin its descent downwards through the 1920s to the 1960s. The decades after that would tell a different story.

COMPROMISE AND CIVIL WAR, 1921–1924

For the moment hopes and fears were high concerning what was about to be written in the new chapter on Anglo–Irish relations. Negotiations opened at 11am on 11 October 1921 in 10 Downing Street, London. From the outset it looked like a grossly uneven match. The British team was led by the Prime Minister, the worldly-wise and wily Welsh politician, David Lloyd George, backed up by a formidable group, including Lord Birkenhead, Austen Chamberlain and Winston Churchill. The Irish side was led by the donnish, intellectual Chairman of Dáil Éireann, Arthur Griffith, alongside Michael Collins, the militant rebel who had undermined British intelligence in Ireland but who was a mere twenty-nine years of age. Others in the Irish delegation were Robert Barton, Eamon Duggan and George Gavan Duffy. Erskine Childers was official secretary to the delegation.

Fighting the British from behind local ditches was one thing. Taking on the negotiating might and experience of the British Empire on their home pitch was quite another.

The Irish needed all the weight and skill they could muster and the decision of de Valera to stay at home considerably weakened their hand. De Valera's decision, ostensibly made on the basis that as 'President' of the 'Republic' he should stay above the fray, has remained one of the most contentious issues in modern Irish history. After all, the British delegation was led by their Prime Minister. Whatever de Valera's motivation, and some would see it in the worst light, his action left him free to reject the final Treaty. Further weakness was built into the Irish delegation's position by the apparently contradictory powers given to it. On the one hand the Dáil voted them a free hand in negotiations. But following that vote de Valera issued written instructions that no major or final decisions were to be made in London without their first being submitted to Dublin.

The final 'Articles of Agreement' were signed on 6 December 1921. In the interminable, twisting negotiations the question of Ulster, as always, was the spoiler. The Unionists had already been granted limited autonomy and a local parliament the year before. They had their six-county area, newly styled Northern Ireland, and were more than content to exist firmly under the Crown and subject to Westminster's writ. The IRA had fought on for a total break with the Crown and for the all-Ireland 'Republic'. Clearly these two positions were irreconcilable. Lloyd George was put under severe pressure not to yield to the 'rebels' by selling out on 'loyal' Ulster.

This crunch issue was not so much solved as shelved. The Irish delegation agreed to the British proposal of a Boundary Commission which would determine the borders of Northern Ireland. Irish republicans felt certain this Commission would, in effect, dismember Northern

Ireland, given the nationalist majorities and enclaves in four of those six counties – Armagh, Fermanagh, Derry and Tyrone. This ploy saved Lloyd George's political neck but was to prove yet another bitter disappointment for republicans when, some years later, the entire entity of Northern Ireland was consolidated by the Commission's recommendations.

Behind the inevitable drift to an unpalatable compromise on the 'Republic' lay Michael Collins's view that the IRA had not the capacity to fight another round against the British. Many republicans, including de Valera, had talked about continuing the war if Britain did not yield during the negotiations. But Collins felt that once he had come out to negotiate his cover was blown and with it his capacity to return to an undercover counter-intelligence campaign. More importantly, the IRA was seriously short of weapons and many members had compromised themselves by appearing in public, wearing uniforms. Further, a decision to fight on would inevitably bring the IRA into head-to-head conflict with the northern Unionists who were well-armed and who could rely on powerful British political backing. Breaking the terms of the July truce would be a formidable and risky decision by the IRA leadership. Such an action would free the British military to return to a policy of repression.

Near the end of negotiations Lloyd George made it plain to Michael Collins that bloody war would, indeed, be the outcome if the Irish declined to sign the Articles of Agreement. In another of those divisive and contentious moves which dominated later republican doctrine, Collins, Griffiths and the rest signed in London, leaving themselves open to the charge that they had sold out under duress. However, under the Treaty agreement, the final decision of ratification was left to a vote in Dáil Éireann. This, in turn, led to bitter recriminations between former comrades-in-arms and, ultimately, to civil war.

As the terms of the negotiations ensured from the outset, the Irish delegation had not secured a Republic. Nor had they provided an all-Ireland state. It was to be an 'Irish Free State', virtually independent but under the Crown: a 'stepping stone' to the Republic, as Collins famously argued. The bitterest pill for many was contained in Clause 4, the oath to be taken by members of the pro-posed new State's parliament. The oath was paraded by its detractors as as an oath of allegiance to the Crown. It wasn't quite that. Members would swear:

> ... true faith and allegiance to the constitution of the Irish Free State (and be) faithful to H.M. King George V, his heirs and succes-sors by law, in virtue of the common citizenship of Ireland with Great Britain and her adherence to and membership of the group of nations forming the British Commonwealth of Nations.'

In theory the Irish Free State covered the whole island. But, under the Agreement, Northern Ireland was given freedom to opt out, which predictably it did. What was left, the twenty-six county area, had won the same autonomy as Canada, Australia, New Zealand and South Africa. It was a huge triumph for the Irish republican cause, given where that cause stood when the small defeated band of insur-gents were laughed off Dublin's streets back in 1916. For many, however, the sacrifices of the intervening years were for one goal only. For these people the Articles of Agreement were a betrayal too far. They would fight on. On 7 January 1922, Dáil Éireann voted by 64 to 57 to ratify the Agreement, formalising it as a binding Treaty. Michael Collins stayed to build upon the 'stepping stone' to the

Republic. De Valera led a walk-out.

Although many who walked out were destined to fight on for a thirty-two county Republic, the reality was that de Valera himself had been prepared to settle for something a good deal short of that. The difference between the Treaty and de Valera's counter-proposal, known as Document Number Two, was thin enough. Yet, in walking out of Dáil Éireann, de Valera helped to propel the country into a violent civil war, which poisoned Irish politics for more than half a century afterwards. Document Number Two proposed a 'Treaty of Association between Ireland and the British Commonwealth'. Crucially, there was no proposed oath declaring faithfulness to the Monarch. But Clause 6 of de Valera's proposal said that 'for the purposes of the Association, Ireland shall recognise His Britannic Majesty as head of the Association'. As for Northern Ireland, de Valera's Document explicitly ruled out force or coercion and proposed that Northern Ireland be granted the same privileges and safeguards as were enshrined in the Treaty which he had rejected.

In practice, de Valera found himself halfway between the supporters of the Treaty and the out-and-out militarists. These were mostly young activists who were determined to fight and die for the Republic to which they had sworn allegiance: men like Liam Lynch, Rory O'Connor, Liam Mellowes, Tom Barry, Seán MacBride and Peadar O'Donnell, names to fill the ensuing pages of militant Irish republican history. De Valera's 'Association' with the British Commonwealth would not satisfy these men. These were the men who sporadically fought guerrilla actions following the Treaty decision, who formally defied the new Irish Free State's authority and who founded the new Irish Republican Army.

THE IRA REBORN

On 26 March 1922, in defiance of the new government, an IRA Convention was held in Dublin's Mansion House. For the first time, the Irish Republican Army was formally established under a new constitution. It offered its services to the Republican government (that is, the anti-Treaty 'Cabinet' headed by de Valera) and pledged to maintain the independence of the Irish Republic, as established by vote in 1919.

In republican parlance, this body constituted the 'new' IRA. The 'old' IRA were those who fought the War of Independence, an increasing number of whom stayed with Michael Collins and supported the Treaty. Thus began the formal struggle by the 'new' IRA to overthrow the Treaty by military force, a struggle destined to continue right into the 1990s. The enduring constitutional command structure consisting of a General Army Convention, Army Executive and Army Council was set in place. The first Chief-of-Staff of the Army Council was Liam Lynch, a thirty-two year old member of the Supreme Council of the IRB and a leading militant activist in Co Cork. Lynch began an immediate military confrontation with the fledgling Irish Free State.

On 13 April 1922, the new Army Council ordered the occupation of several Dublin buildings and vantage points, the most significant being the judicial power centre, the Four Courts along the River Liffey. By these actions the 'new' IRA was attempting to establish itself as the legitimate army of the Republic. The Irish Free State was entering a dangerous period during which it would either collapse or assert its authority. A general election was called for 10 June, with the prospect of a pact of sorts between former comrades Michael Collins and Eamon de Valera. That notion was to founder in mistrust.

In the meantime, the Four Courts remained under IRA control and, as election day loomed, two further events catapulted the Free State forces into military action. In London two republican activists, assumed to be IRA, assassinated Field Marshal Sir Henry Wilson, former Chief of the Imperial General Staff and then military advisor to the new Northern Ireland Prime Minister, Sir James Craig. In Dublin the IRA kidnapped General O'Connell, Chief-of-Staff of the Free State army. Under severe pressure, particularly from London, President Arthur Griffith ordered a military response. Using borrowed British field guns the Four Courts building was blasted and recovered.

This opened up the gaping wound of the Irish civil war. It was a vicious blood-letting. Comrade fought comrade. But it was a war the IRA lost. The new militarists found that old safe houses were closed to them. They found, too, that in the end Eamon de Valera, the arch-pragmatist and compromiser, would neither follow nor lead them into the wilderness. The Free Staters had already won a sort of popular mandate at the general election, de Valera's anti-Treaty group winning only 36 out of 128 seats. The Free State was intent on making its authority hold and, after a terrible period of repressive measures, it succeeded. A Council of War was formed in July, with Michael Collins appointed Commander-in-Chief of the National Army. Then came a shuddering shock.

On 22 August 1922 in the valley of Béal na mBláth, Co Cork, Michael Collins was killed in an ambush. Collins's death was never properly claimed nor explained but it was one of that period's most emotionally wrenching moments. Still, in the IRA lexicon Collins was marked down as a failure, the man who sold out on the Republic, whose stepping stones led nowhere. Only the unrepentant republicans, those who stayed apart from the troublesome Treaty, were held aloft as true heroes.

At the time, and since, it was the Treatyites who won out. In October 1922 Free State Military Courts were established in law. On 8 December, in reprisals for the assasination of a pro-Treaty member of Dáil Éireann, four IRA leaders were executed, among them Liam Mellowes and Rory O'Connor. More than seventy others were sentenced to execution, their fate held hostage to IRA actions. An eye for an eye was the ruling maxim. Further pressure was heaped upon the IRA leadership when the Roman Catholic bishops condemned IRA actions and their republican oath as morally indefensible. The result was that many IRA activists were refused the sacraments. Hard choices were being forced upon the IRA leadership as the killing, ambushing and bank-raiding continued into 1923. Many men had been fighting more or less continuously since 1919.

What never went away for the republicans was the complicating factor of the north. The IRA could never accept the separateness or the legitimacy of the northern Unionists, could never square their own repeated declarations that the Unionists must not be coerced into an independent Ireland with the IRA's actual physical coercive methods. To many southern IRA leaders the north was a place apart. Northern nationalists, however, found themselves being locked into a Protestant/Unionist sectarian statelet, where all power was vested in the victors. The more southern Ireland pressed for the Republic the more northern Unionists raised their barricades. Keeping the republican fight going in the new Northern Ireland became increasingly futile. IRA actions had intensified there until, in May 1922, the Northern Ireland government moved decisively and interned about 400 men.

By 1923 there was no prospect of destabilising either Northern Ireland or the southern Free State. Nonetheless, IRA Chief-of-Staff Liam Lynch remained defiant, resisting pressure from de Valera and others to call a halt. The Free State government was seeking an IRA surrender, spurning de Valera's attempts to get agreed terms for a ceasefire. A number of IRA executive meetings were held during March and April 1923, aimed at arriving at an agreed way forward and avoiding yet another split. On the way to one decisive IRA Executive meeting on 10 April, Liam Lynch was killed by government troops in Co Tipperary. One of his staunchest allies, Austin Stack, was captured, paving the way for the 'peace group' to win out. Frank Aiken, the new Chief-of-Staff from south Armagh, formed an alliance with de Valera and other 'Cabinet' members and a majority was found for a halt to hostilities. On 30 April 1923 Aiken ordered a suspension of all offensive operations. Three weeks later, on 24 May 1923, came the final halt and a watershed in militant Irish republicanism. Aiken signed an order to 'cease fire and dump arms'. With this came de Valera's admission of defeat. In a powerful message to those who had fought on and those who vowed to fight further, de Valera wrote:

> The Republic can no longer be defended successfully by your arms. Further sacrifice of life would be vain and continuance of the struggle in arms unwise in the national interest and prejudicial to the future of our case. Military victory must be allowed to rest for the moment with those who have destroyed the Republic.

There was more than a hint in Dev's message that the fight would be resumed. But both de Valera himself, along with Aiken and a host of others, were to set out on a purely political course, albeit underscored by a whiff of sulphur. Between them they would form a new 'slightly constitutional' party, Fianna Fáil, vowing, though failing, to secure the Republic by political means. In 1924 the Irish Republican Brotherhood dissolved itself, leaving residual funds lying dormant in a bank account. It was a mean and bitter end to the military struggle which had delivered a divided country, a civil war and a legacy of hatred. Those who stayed outside held on to their Constitution, their oath to the Republic and, above all, to what they regarded as their legitimacy.

FINAL FAILURE,
1924–1944

In the years that followed, the IRA crumbled. Under their Constitution *they* were the Army of the only thirty-two county 'Republic' ever elected: those remaining anti-Treaty members of the 1919–1921 'Cabinet' were the true and legitimate government of that Republic. And so the undiluted republicans waited their moment. Some argued for another round against the British. Some vested their hopes in de Valera. Dev's thirty-six-strong elected group had stayed away from the 'illegal' Free State parliament, refusing to take the detested oath to the British King. The hope was that de Valera would win power, re-establish the Republic and bring the IRA in as its army. As for Sinn Féin it had fragmented under the competing forces of the Civil War. By the time two more general elections had been held, in 1923 and 1927, Sinn Féin's parliamentary strength had collapsed to seven seats. By that stage the Free State was fully entrenched. De Valera's new pragmatic republican party, Fianna Fáil was working the system, including the existing Free State army.

As these developments progressed the great majority of republicans and IRA volunteers followed Dev into the new structures. Some simply faded away. Crunch time, the final failure for the IRA, was delayed until 1936 when de Valera declared the IRA illegal. There could only be one government and one army. Two years later, with a new Constitution passed by popular mandate, the new state was unassailable. Those were bleak days indeed for the IRA faithful. This extraordinary turn of events represented a massive failure and unimaginable disenchantment.

THE ROAD TO DISENCHANTMENT

During all of this, IRA GHQ continued to exist and to meet. For the moment, Frank Aiken was still Chief-of-Staff, vowing like the rest never to give up the struggle. Upwards of 10,000 men were in prison. The Free State President, William Cosgrave and his Minister for Justice Kevin O'Higgins maintained a constant assault on this rival army. Cosgrave also had to contend with serious disaffection from within. Many IRA activists had followed Collins out of loyalty, firm in the belief that his stepping stone of a Free State would, indeed, swiftly lead to the Republic. Some turned their bitter disappointment into action. In March 1924, for instance, an incipient 'mutiny' in the Free State army was snuffed out.

In Northern Ireland order was secured, principally by the locally based part-time constabulary, called the B Specials. As far as northern Unionists were concerned the Free State had gone its own way and separated itself from the United Kingdom. Furthermore, to the horror of nationalist Ireland, the Boundary Commission, set up under the terms of the Treaty to examine the new Border, recommended no changes. The six-county area of Northern Ireland would remain as it was. Northern nationalists, fully expecting release from this Unionist camp, found themselves permanently locked in. Treatyites felt betrayed and vulnerable.

Nonetheless, with a return to war not an option, the Free State government signed the Confirmation of Amending Agreement Act in December 1925 confirming existing boundaries. This move represented a massive failure for the 'stepping stone' republicans and a major rallying point for de Valera. But Dev, too, had ruled out coercing the northern Unionists. And as far as they were concerned, the Border was now signed, sealed and delivered. The only united Ireland Unionists would contemplate would be the return of southern Ireland to the United Kingdom fold.

Meanwhile the IRA had been attempting a re-organisation. In June 1925 a new republican newspaper *An Phoblacht* was launched, under the direction of Peadar O'Donnell, who was trying unsuccessfully to steer the IRA towards full-blooded socialism. In November that year the IRA held a Convention in Dalkey, Co Dublin. All the new fissures came to the surface. Under debate was Frank Aiken's New Direction proposal, suggesting a less militaristic approach to the new situation, even opening up the prospect of entering the 'illegal' Free State Dáil. After all, the 'dump arms' order had remained in force and there was no war to fight. In the end the militarists won much of the day. They defeated Aiken's resolution, got a hardliner, Andy Cooney, installed as Chief-of-Staff and decided by vote that the IRA Executive, not the so-called 'Cabinet' should have the power to declare war. Yet another band of young Turks felt *they* could finish the business. Yet another drift away and a split became inevitable.

While the new militarists, with no war to fight, began

41

quasi-military activities like springing volunteers from prison, de Valera was making political moves. On 11 March 1926, Dev resigned as President of Sinn Féin, taking with him such former IRA leaders as Seán Lemass, Seán T O'Kelly and Seán McEntee. A month later, on 17 April, 'Fianna Fáil, the Republican Party' was publicly announced. Its inaugural meeting took place in the La Scala Theatre, Dublin, on 16 May. To the utter dismay of many volunteers, Frank Aiken joined the new party. De Valera's moves proved dramatically successful. In the 1927 (June) general election Fianna Fáil won 44 seats to Cosgrave's Cumann na nGael, 47, the rest being divided across a number of smaller parties. Dev's supporters refused to take the Oath and were refused entry. In this confrontational and destabilising atmosphere, Minister for Justice O'Higgins was shot dead. Cosgrave's government then passed a law requiring all candidates to take the oath if elected. This was followed by a second general election. Still on a determinedly anti-Treaty ticket Fianna Fáil made further gains. They won 57 seats, with pro-Treaty Cumann na nGael, taking 62. De Valera then led his party into Dáil Éireann, and to cries of sell-out from the unrepentant IRA outside, took the dreaded oath.

The battle-lines for the rest of the 20th century were now drawn. These were *political* not military lines. For many former militarists the good days were starting anew. De Valera *was* delivering the goods, promising the all-Ireland Republic by political means. Fianna Fáil defeated Cumann na nGael in the 1932 election and, with the help of the Labour Party, formed a government. De Valera immediately abolished the Oath of Allegiance. Another election in 1933 and another in 1937 left Fianna Fáil as the dominant political party in the Free State, the party of government. In between, de Valera's government opened up an 'economic war' with Britain and began unravelling the Free State.

By this stage the IRA's days as a force to be reckoned with were numbered. They had contemplated and planned a rising against the Cosgrave government. But by resolving to campaign against Cosgrave during elections they had tacitly supported de Valera in his pursuit of power. Once in power, however, de Valera made it plain that no section of the Irish people would be allowed to arm in opposition to the state. Seeking a mission, the IRA, now under Chief-of-Staff Moss Twomey, went into further division. Opposing Twomey's traditional militant republicanism, Peadar O'Donnell led the attempt to pull them leftwards into political activism, towards radical social and economic change.

During 1936 the IRA north and south was dealt a series of body blows. In April that year the Royal Ulster Constabulary swooped on an IRA session, called to consider the failure of an arms raid in Belfast, and arrested virtually the entire northern leadership. Among the arrested was Twomey's right-hand man, Jim Killeen. South of the Border de Valera made a decisive move against the very existence of the IRA. His action followed a number of IRA activities, in particular the killing in Castletownshend, Co Cork, of seventy-two year old former British Vice-Admiral Henry Boyle Somerville. In May 1936 Twomey was arrested and sentenced for subversion against the state. On 18 June 1936, de Valera's government declared the IRA an illegal organisation.

In parallel, de Valera was proving his credentials as a republican. During 1937 his government carried a new Constitution by referendum. This Constitution renamed the state 'Éire' or 'Ireland'. Articles 2 and 3, claimed the whole thirty-two counties as the national territory though Dáil Éireann's jurisdiction would cover only the twenty-six county area, pending the re-integration of the national territory. These Articles placed 'Éire' in legal conflict with Northern Ireland and gave some considerable comfort to the abandoned northern nationalists. Articles 2 and 3 were also designed, in part, to remove the last vestiges of justification for force in pursuing the 'Republic'. However, they also gave full constitutional recognition to Dáil Éireann, as established by the Treaty of 1922. To the recalcitrant but fast diminishing number of IRA activists and anti-Treatyites, this recognition represented the ultimate sell-out. This, in turn, led to a major shift, a shift which left the IRA in direct confrontation with the southern state throughout the following decades.

A small number of the Executive or 'Cabinet' of the Second Dáil of 1921 were still alive. In their own parlance they were still the legal government of the 'Republic' and the IRA still its army. As they watched Fianna Fáil take a grip on the existing institutions, these Executive members, in accordance with a resolution passed in the heady days of 1919, decided to hand over the powers of government to the Army Council of the IRA. This was done in Dublin on 8 December 1938. The seven Executive members who signed over this power were: Mary MacSwiney (widow of the dead hunger-striker Terence MacSwiney), Thomas Maguire, Charles Murphy, Professor Stockley, George Noble Count Plunkett, Brian O'Higgins and JJ 'Sceilg' Kelly. From that point on the IRA Army Council took to itself the entire mantle of the 'Republic' as elected in 1919–1921. *They* were the true government. It was that which gave them their 'moral superiority' and their right to take up arms.

TARGETTING BRITAIN

Diminished and underground as it was, the IRA was set to become more focused, though not without yet more division. Moss Twomey, who had lost rank when imprisoned, would oppose the new tactic about to be agreed and turned his attention to running a grocery business in Dublin. Those who remained were finally free of de Valera's apron strings. They knew their mission – to achieve a final British withdrawal from Ireland – though they would remain divided on the methods to be employed.

The Army Council was now under Chief-of-Staff Seán Russell, a veteran of the 1916 Rising who had split from de Valera over the formation of Fianna Fáil. His was the uncompromising 'Brits out' anti-socialist brand of Irish republicanism. Another of Russell's opponents, the lawyer Seán MacBride, was also moved to leave the IRA in dissension and after the War went on to form a new republican political party, Clann na Poblachta. For now, Russell's group had the leadership and against this internal dissent, the Army Council decided on a campaign in Britain itself. With that in mind they would make a formal 'declaration of war' against Great Britain. This would be organised from GHQ in Dublin. Activists and equipment were put in place. On 12 January 1939 the Army Council's declaration was sent to the British Foreign Secretary, Lord Halifax, demanding a full withdrawal of British forces and government personnel from Ireland. Four days later came seven substantial explosions in electrical power plants in London, Birmingham, Manchester and elsewhere. Security clamp-downs were interspersed with a series of other bombings, including the London Underground.

With Britain pre-occupied with the coming war, the IRA, as with past Irish separatist groups, looked to Britain's enemy for assistance. Lines were opened through a German agent in Dublin. Seán Russell sent an IRA representative to Hamburg for a series of meetings, which seemed to promise a good supply of arms and radio equipment. In the end, nothing came of it and the IRA turned its attention to the United States for cash to sustain its 'war' against Great Britain. Half a year into the British campaign the IRA had hit dozens of targets with a variety of explosive devices, including banks, post offices and cinemas, causing injuries not deaths. In Dublin de Valera's government was outraged by the IRA actions, carried out in the name of the 'Government of Ireland'. As de Valera had repeatedly said there would be only one government and one army. His government began an exceptionally tough crackdown on the IRA using military courts to deal expeditiously with the threat.

De Valera came to pursue a tightrope policy of friendly neutrality towards Britain during World War II. At the same time he was spearheading an anti-Partition propaganda drive against the existence of Northern Ireland. He had to avoid trampling too much on republican sentiment. The IRA, however, gave him the necessary excuse for the toughest response to their British campaign. On 25 August 1939 a major IRA explosion in Coventry killed five and injured more than sixty people. Squeezed now by harsh British police sweeps and Irish military courts, IRA GHQ looked like being totally undermined. In addition, the American fund-raising drive faltered. Then came an amazing sequence of events beginning with an astonishingly brazen IRA operation.

On 23 December 1939 IRA units successfully opened up the Irish Army's reserves of arms at the Magazine Fort in Dublin's Phoenix Park. They got away with around a dozen lorry loads of weapons, including a million rounds of ammunition. But successful and audacious as the exploit was, this amount of weaponry posed huge logistical problems for the IRA. They simply were not prepared for it and could not cope with the job of hiding it securely. Extensive follow-up sweeps by the Irish police not only recovered most of the stolen arms but brought in large numbers of other weapons and equipment, seriously interrupting the IRA's underground networks and undermining the IRA campaign in Britain. In January 1940, de Valera's government won parliamentary approval for extensive new emergency powers. With this they interned IRA leaders and activists. This matched an earlier internment move in Northern Ireland.

In a strange twist, Seán Russell himself had died back in August 1939 on a German U-boat en route to Ireland from America via Italy and Germany. In his absence the British campaign withered and died. So too did renewed actions in the North, being carried on under a largely separate Northern Command. Belfast commander Tom Williams was hanged for the killing of a policeman and, in the south, the then IRA Chief-of-Staff, Charlie Kerrins was hanged for a similar offence. So damaging was this attrition that, by War's end, the IRA effectively ceased to exist. The normal passing on of power from Army Convention to Army Executive to Army Council had been breached and broken. Little was left but faded dreams, unfulfilled ambitions and ageing or disenchanted exinternees. To cap this rout of militant Irish republicanism, Fianna Fáil emerged with major popular support, having won a clear overall majority in Dáil Éireann in the 1944 general election. De Valera's brand of constitutional republicanism appeared renewed, triumphant and vindicated.

RE-IGNITING THE FLAME, 1944–1961

It seemed crystal clear to all and sundry that a corner had been turned in Irish history. In Dublin de Valera's government had emerged from 'The Emergency', as World War II was called south of the Border, with its pride intact and its hold on the republican high ground complete. The entity of Northern Ireland, however, was also more entrenched despite de Valera's anti-Partition campaign at home and abroad. Few could predict how verbal republicanism would change all of that, particularly as the north's loyal stand during the War had won new allies for the Unionists at Westminster.

One thing could be said with apparent certainty – the IRA was a spent force, a thing of history. Fianna Fáil, the Republican Party, had seen them off. The faithful themselves, in and out of prison, would have said so too. Yet, against all the odds, in spite of the chill winds blowing, the flame *was* re-ignited. Spluttering and falteringly to begin with, the IRA torch was eventually rekindled by a tough band of dedicated activists who filled another chapter with anticipation, action and partial success but also with division and, ultimately, failure. All of this occurred over the period 1945 to 1962. It involved the total reconstitution of the IRA, its realignment with Sinn Féin and a military offensive along the Border. In the end, failure or not, the IRA remained in being.

BUILDING A CENTRE

Without a list of names or IRA records, without an Executive or Army Council, it seemed impossible to know where to start. And precious few had any interest in starting. But one day in 1945, in O'Neill's pub in Pearse Street, Dublin, a meeting was arranged, using stolen Garda intelligence to decide whom to invite. Among the small band of instigators were Tony Magan, Willie McGuinness and Cathal Goulding, each with varying militant backgrounds and each to play a large part in the long-haul reconstruction of the IRA. Out of the meeting in O'Neill's pub came a provisional staff for a new Dublin Brigade with McGuinness as Commanding Officer. It was a start, but without an IRA Executive and Army Council this disparate and irrelevant group had no legitimacy and no future.

The last Executive was formed back in 1938 when Seán Russell took control. That was before World War II, before the IRA's British campaign, an age away. Yet through various contacts the Executive's remaining members were traced and requested to confer the required legitimacy. With co-options, five existing members permitted a full twelve member Executive to be formed. This body in turn appointed an Army Council which then appointed a Chief-of-Staff, Paddy Fleming, ex-internee and activist from the British campaign. Theoretically, the 'Declaration of War' against Great Britain, which launched that campaign six years previously, was still in being. Setting the record straight, Fleming's Army Council, on 10 March 1945, called a ceasefire with Great Britain.

To the outside world these manoeuverings went totally unnoticed and would have looked pretty ludicrous, much like the seemingly preposterous Proclamation by the self-styled Army of the Republic back in 1916. But the IRA has been a stickler for continuity and 'legitimacy'. Without these claims they were unable to justify to themselves the use of armed force to win back the Republic. Conversely, with this assumed legitimacy almost any means could be justified to achieve that objective. As always the 'means' meant armed physical force, guns, ammunition and explosives, trained activists, a military command structure plus a military strategy. It would be a full eleven years before those elements were properly in place and a new campaign launched.

For the moment, in bleak 1945, the dedication of the faithful was being tested, particularly as the Special Branch police in Dublin began taking an interest, leading to the imprisonment of some of the organisers. There were also the bitter residues of the divisions over the British campaign and the in-fighting among internees in the Curragh Camp. Between one thing and another, more time was lost, taking events to 1947. After yet another re-organisation and a new Army Council, Willie McGuinness was appointed Chief-of-Staff and a recruitment drive got underway.

In between came a new split within militant Irish republicanism. When Seán MacBride and others formed the Clann na Poblachta political party, preparing like de Valera before them to 'sell out' and take their seats in Dáil Éireann, the IRA responded by expelling those who joined the new party. The result was to retain the IRA's 'purity' but also to reduce greatly its base of support. The Clann appeared to be sweeping all before it at large public meetings, winning two by-elections, then winning an astonishing ten seats in the February 1948 general election, promising to replace Dev's verbal republicanism with the real thing. It was rough terrain all over again for the IRA. But the ground expanded somewhat when MacBride's party formed an unlikely coalition with Labour and the hated 'Free-Staters', Fine Gael.

During 1947 and 1948 Cathal Goulding ran training

camps in the Wicklow hills, a new journal called the *United Irishman* was launched and another Army Convention made yet more changes. This time the platform for the tedious reconstruction was properly built. The new Chief-of-Staff was Tony Magan, a tough, disciplined military organiser. Into the frame came two veteran activists, Thomas MacCurtain, son of the legendary Mayor of Cork killed by the RIC in 1920, and Paddy McLogan, a traditional militant republican of standing, with a history dating back before 1916. These three men formed the bedrock of the new IRA. The Convention of September 1948 passed two resolutions, empty of reality but with significant future resonances. They resolved a) to launch a military campaign in the north and b) to take no military action against the southern state.

The next year, 1949, saw another development, also to become significant over time. Sinn Féin and the IRA re-formed their alliance, Sinn Féin accepting that the IRA Army Council held the powers of the government of the Republic and as such was the 'supreme authority'. Infiltration and control of Sinn Féin became IRA policy and in 1950 Paddy McLogan was elected Sinn Féin President. Within the IRA Tony Magan set about stamping his authority on the organisation, at times forcing out some of its most dedicated people, including Willie McGuinness, and winning broad if grudging support for his harshest disciplinary actions.

Future battle-lines had been further drawn when, on Easter Monday 1949, the new coalition government, led by John A Costello, declared Ireland to be a Republic, with Dáil Éireann retaining jurisdiction over the twenty-six county area. Westminster followed this by copper-fastening Northern Ireland's status in law. The new IRA of

Magan, MacCurtain and McLogan now well and truly had a cause. They were out on their own, the only organisation with the mission to take the torch of the 1919 all-Ireland Republic and run with it. In May 1951 the IRA established a Military Council with the defined aim of drawing up a campaign plan, based on the resolution of 1948, to fight for the north. The centre had been built. As a military outfit, however, the IRA were still of little consequence, still only patchily organised, still riven with self-doubt and still without the tools for the job. The next long-haul task would be to acquire arms. Though most recruits would scarcely have been happy to know it, actual fighting was five years away.

ACQUIRING THE TOOLS

From 1951 to 1955 the IRA engaged in a number of meticulously planned raids for arms, while the Military Council gradually put detail on the resolution to take on the British presence in Northern Ireland. On 3 June 1951 the re-constituted Derry Brigade got permission for an audacious arms raid. It was a complete success. With inside assistance the raiders penetrated the armoury of the Territorial Army in the Joint Royal Navy/RAF Anti-Submarine School within Ebrington British Army barracks. The IRA party got away with 12 modern service rifles, 20 Sten guns and 8 machine guns with matching ammunition. The northern authorities were surprised and unprepared, given the lengthy period of IRA inactivity. RUC intelligence had got no wind of it. The B-Specials were merely on a stand-by reserve basis, understrength and with ageing County Commanders.

The raid gave the IRA a big logistics and propaganda success. Its public profile and recruitment prospects were enhanced. All good stuff for the new leadership. This, in turn, strengthened the Army Council's hand against a number of rival militant republican groups, some of whom, like the general populace, were until then unaware of the IRA's re-emergence. Tony Magan's men set about absorbing these groups into the re-constituted Republican movement of the IRA and Sinn Féin. Some, like Liam Kelly's Saor Uladh paramilitary group in east Tyrone, remained resistant to the IRA's bear hug and stayed aloof, ready to take their own action.

Magan's main focus held firmly on his slow and careful preparations for the Border campaign to come. On 25 July 1953 came another high profile arms raid, a similar story but without the happy ending. This time the target was in England, the British Army's Officer's Training Corps School at Felsted in Essex. Magan himself took the lead in its planning. The three men assigned to the job were Cathal Goulding, Manus Canning, from the successful Derry unit, and Seán Stephenson, a London-based ex-RAF man. (Stephenson later re-emerged as MacStiofáin, first Chief-of-Staff of the Provisional IRA, Goulding being on the other side of that particular split.) The raid at Felsted was a triumph turned into disaster. The three-man raiding party got in, loaded up an old van with more than a hundred modern weapons and drove away. But the old, inappropriate, laden-down vehicle was fortuitously stopped by police some miles away. The three ended up with eight year prison sentences in England. It was a major loss in terms of morale and a serious setback for Tony Magan's plans. Unnecessary energy would be spent trying to spring Goulding from prison. Caution was the watchword as other plans for arms raids ran into the sand.

SUCCESS

Then luck turned. On 12 June 1954 came a huge guns harvest, the result of detailed planning and infiltration. The target was the armoury of the Royal Irish Fusiliers at Gough Barracks in Armagh. Using a nineteen-man raiding party, for action inside and outside the barracks, the IRA scored a complete success. No shot was fired, eighteen soldiers were left tied up and the raiders got away with more than 250 rifles, 30 Sten guns, nine Bren light machine guns and 40 training rifles. They had left without taking with them any matching ammunition and this led to further operations down the line.

The raid itself left the Northern authorities floundering. The general alarm was given so late that the B Specials were called out after the raiders had crossed the Border. Stormont's response was to give the police in Northern Ireland more powers of search under the Special Powers Act. The security net tightened and this had its effects later. For the IRA the arms raid yielded a huge propaganda harvest. Funds flowed in from the United States, where one fundraising event auctioned the keys of the gates and armoury of Gough Barracks.

DEBACLE

Just as the tide began to flow in favour of the IRA it ebbed again. Another arms raid four months later in October turned into a miserable failure with serious losses. Again the plan involved infiltration of a barracks complex, this time the Royal Inniskilling Fusiliers armoury at Omagh, Co Tyrone. On 16 October 1954, a total of thirty men was sent north by GHQ in Dublin. The prize, every bit as impressive as that in Gough barracks, was hundreds of modern weapons. But the operation went desperately awry, particularly when a sentry was knifed. In the evacuation and consequent shooting several IRA men were injured. In the hunt, this time involving a full call-out of B-Specials, eight men were arrested, including the O/C of the operation. Magan himself, who had been based in Monaghan for the job, managed to get in and out of Northern Ireland undetected when the raiding party failed to rendezvous as planned. The Omagh debacle led to intensified interest in the IRA on the part of the Special Branch in Dublin in case the southern state itself might be on Tony Magan's target list. This further concentrated minds on the Army Council and out of the post mortem following Omagh came Standing Order No 8. The Order said:

> Volunteers are strictly forbidden to take any military action against the 26 County forces under any circumstances whatsoever ... [and they] ... must make it clear that the policy of the Army is to drive the British Forces of Occupation out of Ireland.

This set a new long-term pattern for IRA actions. Unlike in the civil war period, the south would be used solely for training, planning and arms dumps. The north would be the 'war zone'. This policy had its twisted logic too in that the '26 County forces', like the other institutions of the southern state, were regarded by the IRA as illegal and treasonable, just as much the enemy as the northern institutions. Pragmatically, this policy allowed the IRA in the 1950s, as later, to target the north without having to watch their backs too much.

For the moment, targetting the north still meant raiding for arms and reversing the recent blow to morale. Omagh Mark 2 was planned for 5 March 1955, using a fifty man team. But ambitions were thwarted and Omagh Mark 2 was aborted at the last minute due to extensive RUC and B-Specials activity.

TRIUMPH

Still, the various events of recent years had hugely enhanced the profile and standing of the IRA and the republican cause. Perversely, as always, logistical failure could be turned to propaganda and fund-raising success, as happened with the trials of those arrested after the Omagh raids. One man, in particular, Tom Mitchell, became a *cause célèbre.*

When it came to the Westminster Elections of 26 May 1955 the re-aligned IRA/Sinn Féin felt sufficiently confident to put up candidates. Sinn Féin activists had been working away on the ground in the nationalist areas, building up their organisation in competition with the somewhat debilitated Nationalist Party. In the end, after a good deal of pressure, Sinn Féin was given a clear run in the election. They got two men elected, one being the imprisoned Tom Mitchell. But their popular vote was the striking feature of the election. Sinn Féin got more than 152,000 votes or almost the entire nationalist electorate. This was far ahead of anything Sinn Féin could later muster even in the heady days of the early 1980s and mid-1990s. This electoral triumph and the armed ambitions of the IRA combined to raise expectations that the dream could actually be fulfilled, that another round against 'the British Forces of Occupation' could deliver the Republic.

FIGHTING TIME

The next year, 1956, was a busy one. The Military Council's Campaign Plan was sharply focused. Dublin GHQ, which would direct the operation, sent units into the North to prepare the way. The planned date, 11 November 1956 was delayed by a month due to the armed actions of splinter republican groups along the Border. Liam Kelly's Saor

Uladh combined with another disaffected group, recently split from the IRA's Dublin Brigade.

The IRA's Border Campaign proper began, on the night of 11/12 December 1956. Despite the warnings of the earlier arms raids the northern authorities were again taken by surprise. IRA units attacked with guns and explosives, sometimes successfully, sometimes not. They destroyed the BBC's relay station at Rosemount, near Derry; blew up the new Territorial Army depot being built at Enniskillen and set fire to the County Courthouse in Magherafelt. Attempts to blow up three bridges over Lough Erne in Co Fermanagh left two of them damaged but serviceable while the third bomb failed to detonate. The party sent to blow up Gough Barracks in Armagh alerted the sentries, though the fleeing men got safely back across the Border. More attacks followed the next day, 13 December, on RUC stations at Lisnaskea and Derrylin in Co Fermanagh. Roads, bridges and telephone lines were blown up.

It was all heady, headline stuff, designed to show real intent. It also brought swift responses from the northern and southern governments. On 15 December regulations providing for internment without trial were re-introduced in Northern Ireland. A day later came a serious body blow to the secretive command lines set up for 'Operation Harvest', as the IRA campaign was known. The Irish police and army discovered and raided the IRA's operational HQ, a well-hidden farmhouse at Knockatallon, Co Monaghan. The command leaders, though released without evidence, were clearly identified and had to scatter. Some days later a failed attack on Brookeborough RUC station in Co Fermanagh left two IRA men, Seán South and Feargal O'Hanlon, dead. Both men, particularly South, swiftly became new republican martyrs, the subjects of heroic ballads and commemorations.

Emotion was one thing, operational matters quite another. In mid-January a series of sweeps by the southern police took out of action and into prison almost all of the Army Council and GHQ staff, including Tony Magan and Thomas MacCurtain. A temporary Army Council was activated and the campaign continued sporadically, with limited control from Dublin.

The IRA's renewed campaign and Dublin's strong response, however, had put huge strains on the Republic's Coalition government. This, combined with severe austerity measures to deal with economic recession, led to Seán MacBride's republican party, Clann na Poblachta, bringing down the government. The Dáil was dissolved on 12 February 1957 and a general election held on 5 March. The result was a tumult of political fortunes. Fianna Fáil returned to power, Clann na Poblachta lost two-thirds of their vote and Sinn Féin made a big impact, getting almost 66,000 votes and four seats (which they refused to take under their policy of abstention). The effect of this political turnaround was highly significant. The significance was not just Sinn Féin's showing, though that was important; it was the return to power of Fianna Fáil, with its strength and unity and de Valera's republican credentials to crush the IRA as they had done during the War.

IRA heads had not dropped just yet. During the next month, April, the organisation's leaders came out after their six-month prison sentences. Power was returned to the old hands – Magan the Chief-of-Staff, and Robert Russell (nephew of Seán Russell) the Quartermaster General. The campaign continued, somewhat stutteringly. But before it could get into gear again, the IRA inflicted another serious wound and setback on themselves. On 4 July the IRA killed an RUC officer and wounded another in an attack in Forkhill, south Armagh. De Valera's government took its chance and, capitalising on outraged public opinion, introduced internment. Garda sweeps on 6 July rounded up more than sixty activists, taking away the leadership for the second time in six months.

Strategically, the IRA had blundered. In the south there was some support for blowing up British Army bases, a good deal of sympathy for IRA 'martyrs' but virtually none for IRA killing missions, particularly those mounted from the southern side of the Border as the Forkhill one had been. From this point on the IRA was on the defensive. With hindsight it could be said that failure was now inevitable, though the tenacity and determination of the IRA mindset made it a long and difficult slog for the authorities on both sides of the Border.

A renewed winter campaign for 1957–1958 ran into the mud. In the north, sporadic attacks without apparent central control continued to worry the RUC and B-Specials. By October 1957, fifty-one men had been convicted for IRA activities and by December 167 were interned. The new year, 1958, began with increased IRA activity, twenty-five incidents of varying seriousness occurring during January. Roads and bridges were blown up and localised areas of resistance were capable of mounting successful operations.

During 1957 and 1958 Eamon de Valera as Taoiseach made a number of statements refuting the IRA's justification of force to end Partition. De Valera was acutely conscious of the fingers being pointed at the men of his generation, who had fought firstly against the British and, secondly against the Free State government, all in the name of the same Republic. Speaking at the Fianna Fáil Árd Fheis (annual conference) in November 1957, de Valera claimed, with a touch of historical amnesia, that the difference between then and now was that all the armed actions of his generation were governed by a democratic mandate, even if acquired after the event. He declared:

> I was elected, and every action of the Republican Army was taken, as an action of the army authorised by the Government of the Republic.

About the current IRA leaders he said:

> They can find no basis for their present action in the years from 1919 to 1921, nor can they find it in the Civil War. In 1916, it is true, those who went out and proclaimed the Republic could not say that they had positive proof that they had behind them at that time the will of the majority of the people. When I went to Clare in 1917 [where he was elected in a by-election] I said what I wanted the people of Clare to do – and what the people of Clare, thank God, did – was to prove, post factum, that the people who went out in 1916 did represent the will of the people.

Whatever about self-serving historical justifications, de Valera was insisting that the only sovereign Irish government with the power to authorise force was the one over which he presided. In July 1958 he told the Dáil:

> 'There is no authority for the use of force outside the authority that is derived from this House. There can be but one government and one army in this country if it is going to last.'

The IRA, however, totally disregarded de Valera's missives, the Army Council having long since taken to itself the 'powers of government' of the 1919 Republic. As Dev spoke, during July 1958, the armed campaign went up a gear, with thirteen explosions and one RUC constable shot dead. A re-organisation of the IRA leadership had occurred, with a new Chief-of-Staff. The new Army Council decided on a shift of plan, targetting a defined area around Co Fermanagh rather than continuing with a thinly spread offensive. It was a measure of the IRA's reduced ambitions. Several attempts to get enhanced firing power failed, including an operation to 'liberate' rocket launchers from a base in Baldford in Dorset, England.

Then the leadership was taken away yet again. In late September 1958 the Irish police discovered the IRA leadership's clandestine meeting-place, a house in Serpentine Avenue, Dublin. Those arrested included the Chief-of-Staff, a huge loss in the circumstances. Some relief was forthcoming when, on 27 September, two leading activists, men who would stamp their names on much later events, escaped from the Curragh internment camp. They were Ruairí Ó Brádaigh and Dave O'Connell. Two days later a weakened Army Council selected the Leitrim activist, John Joe McGirl, as Chief-of-Staff. These swift changes caused considerable confusion and internal tensions, resulting in broken lines of communication and lost contacts north of the Border, all of which hindered operations. Then another change at the top: on 24 October Ruairí Ó Brádaigh was installed as Chief-of-Staff. His would be the regime that would finally bring 'Operation Harvest' to a halt, though not without further internal turbulence.

For instance, when the Curragh internees were released by de Valera's government in early 1959, Tony Magan and Thomas MacCurtain attempted to resume a leadership role and ultimately lost a divisive drawn-out internal battle. The torch had moved to a new generation. As events moved into 1960 the campaign was all but devoid of anything but the salvaging of honour. Nonetheless the Army Convention of June 1960 took the decision to fight on. More blowing up of roads and custom posts led to more police sweeps.

The Irish general election of 4 October told the story of the faltering military and political campaign. Sinn Féin's popular vote was almost halved, the party losing all four of its seats. It was a time of change in Ireland as well as throughout the industrialised world. The IRA campaign seemed entirely out of tune with an emerging, more confident Republic's *de facto* acceptance of its restricted political territory. This change was mirrored by the coming to the Fianna Fáil leadership of Seán Lemass, who formed a minority government. Lemass, like de Valera, had opposed in arms the Treaty which established the state over which he now presided. He had fought in the GPO during the 1916 Rising and was part of the IRA garrison which occupied Dublin's Four Courts building during the IRA's early strike against the Free State, back in 1922. Now, almost forty years on, the new Taoiseach was about to make an early mark on the latest IRA activists, men fighting Lemass's old fight.

Again the Irish government was assisted by the IRA's own actions. On 12 November 1961 they killed an RUC officer and wounded three others in another south Armagh attack, this time at Jonesboro'. Public outrage allowed Lemass to re-introduce the Military Tribunals, last used to smash the IRA's British campaign in the 1940s. The Tribunals began handing out long sentences. With morale and conviction hit hard and funds drying up, the end came by decision of the Army Council on 3 February 1962 and publicly announced on 26 February. The order went out to dump arms, yet again, for another day.

By the standards of the later campaign this one had a tiny number of casualties: twelve killed in total, six RUC and six IRA (four in one premature explosion), with thirty-eight wounded all round. More than half of the IRA's attack operations occurred in the first thirteen months of the campaign. 'Operation Harvest' made no more than a dent on the British presence in Northern Ireland. The northern authorities seized a huge arsenal, 367 weapons, much of the fruits of all those years of meticulous and laboured preparations. In the end, IRA morale was desperately low. They had been decisively defeated, many unresolved divisions remained, and an uncertain future beckoned. Yet in their own terms they could proudly say one thing. The flame had been kept alive. The IRA was still there.

THE NEW SPLIT,
1960–1972

The 1960s was a period of great optimism, economic advancement, and progressive political change. Internationally the so-called Cold War continued but had somewhat thawed. Stalinism was being moderated in the Soviet Union while, in the United States, President John Kennedy represented something exciting and new. Civil rights and religious ecumenism came centre stage. Youth was winning its place and pride. Old hatchets were being buried in western Europe as the ambitious European Economic Community took hold. In Britain the Labour Party replaced the crusty and tired Tories. There, a brash new Prime Minister, Harold Wilson, promised the white heat of a technological revolution. In Ireland, north and south, mental and psychological borders began coming down.

Making history, the old IRA leader and Taoiseach, Seán Lemass, swapped visits with the landed Unionist gent and

Northern Ireland Prime Minister, Terence O'Neill. Neither Unionist nor Republican worlds immediately caved in as a result.

The IRA, seemingly irrelevant to all of this modernisation, was in turmoil, searching for a role. When they thought they had found one – a decisive shift to the left and away from simple militarism – the organisation proved incapable of holding its cohesiveness. As atavistic tribal rivalries were let loose in the latter half of the 1960s the IRA split irrevocably asunder. Out of the tumult came yet another version of the old model, the Provisional IRA, single-minded, fundamentalist, determinedly militaristic.

FINDING A ROLE

The Border Campaign left the IRA divided over its purpose and direction. Tony Magan's group had lost the debilitating internal battle. All three veteran stalwarts of the IRA's rebuilding programme were driven out. Magan himself was finally expelled from the IRA. Thomas MacCurtain had earlier resigned. Patrick McLogan ended up resigning, first as President of Sinn Féin, then as a member of the IRA and eventually, after a Court of Inquiry, he was expelled from Sinn Féin. The row involved two issues. The first concerned policy differences within the IRA's Camp Council in the Curragh Camp during internment (Magan, MacCurtain and McLogan were members of the Council). The second was the Army Council's refusal of a request from Sinn Féin (where McLogan was President and Magan a senior figure) that a statement be issued saying that the Party leadership played no part in the decision to end the Border campaign. It was fractious and legalistic stuff. At root were sharp disagreements, running from 1958 through to 1962, about the conduct of what the IRA called the 'Resistance Campaign' and the manner of the final capitulation.

In the end, the Army Council won the day and firmly laid down its authority, particularly over Sinn Féin. The relationship between the two organisations was enunciated formally by the IRA leadership in April 1964 when the dispute was over. In a four-page, detailed and tightly argued, account of the hiatus, General Headquarters explained how Sinn Féin had accepted its subservience to the IRA since the old relationship was re-established in 1949. The paper gave details of a formal meeting between the IRA and Sinn Féin on 13 May 1962 where the Army Council enunciated the following three-point dictat:

a) That the Army Council was the Government of the Republic and the supreme authority in the Republican Movement.

b) That Sinn Féin is an autonomous and independent organisation but if it wishes to remain within the Republican Movement its policy must conform with Army policy.

c) That no statement be published by Sinn Féin regarding the halting of the Campaign except one supporting the Army Council decision.

From that time onwards the 'supreme authority' of the Army Council has remained intact, Sinn Féin continuing as the 'civil wing' of the Republican movement.

So, back in 1964, the IRA remained in supreme control of the Republican movement. Nonetheless the departure of Magan, MacCurtain and McLogan and a number of other key players, left a disoriented rump behind. Many activists simply faded away, as happened after the British campaign. It would take time but eventually there would grow a new direction and a new leadership. Cathal

Goulding had been released from gaol in England in 1961 and was installed as a somewhat reluctant new Chief-of-Staff in late 1962. Goulding, at least, had the energy and enthusiasm lacking in many others at that low point. It seemed like a small enough change but time would show how significant and divisive the move was. Gradually, around Goulding emerged a small left-wing coterie of individuals inspired more by the doctrines of Karl Marx than those of Wolfe Tone.

During all of this the 'dump arms' order remained in force. The activists had no forseeable mission. The name of the game, for some, became sporadic freelance action. For instance, on St Patrick's Day 1963, an attempt was made to destroy a republican monument in Cork which was being dedicated by de Valera. The effort failed when the explosive device killed one of the two activists and injured the other. For a time a small Munster group, led by Richard Behal, involved themselves in militant skirmishes over unwelcome guests like British royals, Princess Margaret and Lord Snowden in January 1965. Later that year Behal and two others got Army Council approval for an attack on a British Navy vessel coming on an official visit to Waterford. The three ended up with short prison terms for their trouble. Some months later, on 7 March 1966 a splinter group blew up Nelson's Pillar in Dublin's O'Connell Street, the IRA proper having disowned the operation.

This was all sideline action for the Goulding inner circle. During 1964–1965 a number of Marxist theoreticians had come in under the Sinn Féin banner, seeing the organisation as a potential socialist revolutionary force. The most prominent of these recuits was Dr Roy Johnston, an Irish Marxist who had spent time with far left groups in England.

In this period the Wolfe Tone Society was formed, to become a kind of socialist think-tank. Peadar O'Donnell's socialist writings from the 1930s, came back into vogue. The new direction involved infiltration and organisation of protest bodies and battling against foreign landlordism. They particularly honed in on the issue of fishing rights and sought involvement in rural cooperatives along the lines of the early soviets in revolutionary Russia. Out of this came the Republican movement's blueprint for the future, the 'Stages Theory'. This envisaged three evolving stages leading to the overthrow of Irish capitalism.

The straight and basic 'Brits out' militarism of the past was regarded as an out-moded tactic which kept the working-class divided in the north. The aim now would be to develop a powerful and cohesive working class. The 'Stages Theory' saw the first period as the development of a capitalist democracy in Northern Ireland where Protestant and Catholic workers would unite. Stage two, would see the non-sectarian workforces north and south joining together in common cause. The final stage would involve a push against the capitalist edifice across the island, at which point armed struggle might or might not be necessary. It was a programme entirely anathema to those favouring the traditional concept of driving the British out of Ireland with the backing of the Catholic nationalists, followed by the re-establishment of the 1919 all-Ireland Dáil. The new direction would slay other militant republican dragons too. There would be a slow move to actual recognition of Dáil Éireann and the Stormont Parliament, with a view to infiltration and using these chambers as vehicles and platforms in the march to revolutionary socialism. This was a programme for *de-emphasising* the Border rather than raising it in sharp focus.

In this scheme of things the modernisation of Ireland's industrial base through investment by foreign multinationals was a positive thing. It would speed up the necessary education, unionisation and industrialisation of the workforce. To that end also, the effective recognition of Northern Ireland by the Republic, with Seán Lemass's mould-breaking visit to Terence O'Neill in Belfast on 14 January 1965, was not viewed as heresy by these socialist thinkers.

In any event, norther nationalists were becoming more at ease with the Northern Ireland statelet. Two political events in 1965 seemed to settle and consolidate the moves to modernisation, each seemingly weakening the ground for IRA militarism. In November, the North's Prime Minister Terence O'Neill called a general election and won widespread unionist support for his liberalising actions. On the nationalist side, for the first time since Partition in 1920, the Nationalist Party under its leader, Eddie McAteer, took up the role of 'Official Opposition' in the Stormont Parliament.

DARKENING CLOUDS

The rosy garden was also growing weeds which took some time to appear above the blooms before devouring them. For a start, even moderate Unionism, so used to complete political hegemony, was extremely slow to instigate reforms in housing, voting rights and jobs as a response to Eddie McAteer's move at Stormont. Extreme Protestant loyalism was gearing up, especially in the person of a young firebrand preacher from Ballymena called Ian Richard Kyle Paisley. Paisley's new fundamentalist Free Presbyterian Church was established as far back as 1951 but his interest in political action came in the 1960s. Paisley's brand of street politics coincided with the move into political agitation and infiltration by Goulding's IRA. Each would come to rebound off the other.

In 1963 Paisley led a street protest against the lowering of the Union Jack at Belfast's City Hall to mark the death of Pope John XXXIII. During the October 1964 Westminster election Paisley's protest at the flying of the Irish tricolour at Sinn Féin offices on Divis Street, west Belfast, led to serious rioting, leaving 20 police and 50 civilians injured. The visit to Stormont by Seán Lemass greatly fuelled Paisley's bandwagon.

In 1966 there emerged a new militant loyalist body, the Ulster Volunteer Force (taking the name of the populist Unionist UVF which defied Home Rule back in 1912). This new, secretive UVF, with links to established Unionist figures, declared 'war' on the IRA. This came out of the blue at a time when the IRA was moving in the opposite direction and had virtually no public profile at all. However, 1966 was a special year in the republican calendar. It marked the 50th anniversary of the 1916 Rising in Dublin. RUC intelligence had it, wrongly, that the IRA was planning a major offensive to mark the occasion. As it happened the celebrations passed off virtually without incident.

One of the first acts of the UVF 'war' was the killing of innocent Catholics. This led to the arrest and long-term imprisonment of its enigmatic leader, Gusty Spence. The real target of the UVF's political string-pullers, however, was O'Neill's reformism. This was evident when they blew up a number of public utilities and blamed it on the IRA, the intention being to destabilise O'Neill. By the time of the major civil rights protests in the late 1960s the patterns of protest, counter-protest and street agitation were well established and the explosive mix well stirred.

FROM AGITATION TO ARMED ACTION

With civil unrest developing, the Northern Ireland Civil Rights Association (NICRA) was formed in January 1967. Its demands were not British withdrawal or an Irish republic. Among their aims were 'one man one vote' in Council elections, ending gerrymandered electoral boundaries, fair allocation of housing, repeal of Special Powers Act and disbandment of the B-Specials. Unionists and some security intelligence had it that NICRA was an IRA front. Certainly Goulding's Republican Clubs played a part and two members of the Wolfe Tone Society were on NICRA's initial controlling committee. It was clear also that the IRA, under its 'Stages Theory' saw NICRA as a vehicle to advance nonsectarian agitation. NICRA's committee also contained two liberal-minded Unionists as well as trade union and republican labour representatives. When it came to those involved in NICRA's first public demonstration in Dungannon on 24 August 1968, police intelligence chalked up seventy 'republicans', including ten members of the IRA. In an historic NICRA event, a huge march in Derry on 5 October 1968, worldwide TV witnessed vicious batoning by the RUC of the leaders, including elected politicians such as Eddie McAteer and a prominent republican socialist Stormont MP Gerry Fitt.

These were turbulent and unprecedented events. It was virtually impossible to determine the exact role of the IRA. In a British government report on the growing disturbances published in September 1969 the Cameron Commission concluded that while IRA members were involved in NICRA they were not directing or controlling its activities. The reality was that the northern IRA, Belfast Brigade in particular, were sharply critical of the Goulding Army Council's military unpreparedness and its decision to hold back. This Army Council was not about to set course on another traditional 'round' against the British. Northern IRA activists, however, were under severe pressure to 'do something'.

As riots in Derry, Newry, Dungannon, Armagh and Belfast turned into loyalist attacks on Catholic homes, Citizens Defence Committees were formed under the control of a central committee. Members comprised all sorts, including priests and nationalist politicians. Behind the committees the IRA formed a largely unarmed system of auxiliaries. As the 'balloon went up' in late 1969, nationalist leaders of all hues looked to Dublin for support, a major demand being arms for defence. Many guns were handed over by individuals. For many in Fianna Fáil the time had come to put its verbal republicanism into action. Fianna Fáil were in power at this critical juncture but the Taoiseach, Jack Lynch, was the party's first leader not to have come from the old IRA and Treaty times. Lynch's government was riven and split over the demands by some Cabinet ministers like Neil Blaney and Kevin Boland to send the army into the north.

These were days of huge tension, coming close to full-scale civil war and internal insurrection involving the whole island. On the political front Terence O'Neill's position was seriously weakened and his days as Unionist Party leader numbered. Hardline unionism was resisting reform, claiming ever more evidence that the civil rights demands were but a cloak for the real goal of a united Ireland. Ian Paisley's advance gathered powerful momentum. He got close to defeating Terence O'Neill himself in the Stormont Election of February 1969, where twelve of the thirty-nine Unionists elected opposed O'Neill. That was the election which saw the constitutional nationalist baton passed on to a new generation of articulate civil rights activists, where the fifty-five year old Nationalist Party leader, Eddie McAteer, was defeated on his home territory in Derry City by thirty-two year old John Hume. On the nationalist side, at least, the battle lines appeared to be manned by political rather than military activists.

Then unionism shuddered again. Two months later, in April 1969, Terence O'Neill could hold the fort no longer and resigned. He was replaced by another landed gentleman, Major James Chichester-Clark, as the old guard Unionist establishment vainly struggled to retain control. As events cascaded into one another during the latter half of 1969, the B-Specials, in a controversial move, were called into street action, the RUC became exhausted, Harold Wilson's government in London sent in the British Army and a government report into policing recommended major RUC reform and the disbandment of the B-Specials. Loyalism and Paisleyism were enraged at this collapse of their long-standing walls of defence, particularly the demise of the B-Specials who had undoubtedly greatly deterred the IRA's 1956–1962 'Resistance Campaign'.

During all of this Jack Lynch in Dublin responded to the pressure by sending the Irish Army *to* the Border but not *across* it, as many northern nationalists had expected. What *were* sent across the Border into the beleagered nationalist areas were Irish Army intelligence operatives, their major task being to report back to Dublin and to identify those 'safe' republicans, not tainted by the Marxism of the then current IRA leadership. In identifying such individuals, the implicit understanding was that guns would be forthcoming, provided the south was not targetted for armed or revolutionary socialist action. Special Branch in Dublin was fully aware of the IRA's 'Stages Theory' and its long-term objective of overthrowing Irish capitalism, with or without armed force. By then the Army Council had reiterated its decision to push for political agitation rather than military action. The new political vehicle would be a determinedly social-ist and Marxist 'National Liberation Front'. The southern authorities would not be giving the IRA the tools to do that particular job. And so, the split in the IRA was being manipulated from within and without.

The IRA's Belfast Brigade was coming close to mutiny, having demanded armed action from the Army Council and having been repeatedly refused. This disaffection was noted by one of those Irish Army intelligence operatives in Northern Ireland, Capt James Kelly. On 16 September 1969, he reported that the IRA in Dublin 'is not trusted by the Northern Republicans ... the Republicans in the North are willing to go it alone rather than be associated with a Communist-oriented IRA.' Kelly went on to state that the arming of what he termed 'genuine' republicans must be faced, partly to fight an ensuing guerrilla campaign in the north and partly to contain the existing, left-wing, Sinn Féin/IRA programme.

THE IRA SPLITS

On 22 September 1969, the IRA's Belfast Brigade staff was reorganised. New members were taken in and the Brigade then formally disaffiliated from the Army Council. The latest split had started. Meanwhile the organisation of 'safe' and 'genuine' militant republicans went on apace. The final break came at an Army Convention called by the Goulding leadership in December 1969. A majority backed the leader-ship's main proposals: 1) the *de facto* recognition of the gov-ernments in Dublin, Belfast and London by dropping the hallowed IRA policy of abstentionism (not taking seats if elected); 2) the forging of a National Liberation Front as the main vehicle for action. The losing minority then withdrew, held their own General Army Convention and formed a Provisional Army Council. On 28 December 1969 the new group issued a public statement. Stating the reasons for the walk-out it said:

> We declare our allegiance to the 32-County Irish Republic proclaimed at Easter 1916, established by the first Dáil Éireann in 1919, overthrown by force of arms in 1922 and suppressed to this day by the existing British-imposed Six County and 26-County partition states.

> Already a majority of Army Units, individual Volunteers and Republicans generally have given their allegiance to the Provisional Executive and Provisional Army Council elected by us at this convention and have rejected the new compromising leadership in the election of which we did not even participate.

The statement went on to call on members of Sinn Féin to reject the same 'compromising' proposals at its coming Árd Fheis (annual conference).

Three days later, on 31 December 1969, 'legitimacy' was conferred on the new Provisional IRA by the last surviving member of the Executive of the 1921 all-Ireland Dáil, Thomas Maguire. He was one of those Executive members who, in 1938, had 'proclaimed' that the 'Powers of government' were being handed over to the IRA Army Council. The all-important line of legitimacy was kept intact. In his public statement 'Commdt General' Maguire declared that the existing (Goulding) IRA Executive and Army Council were 'illegal'. He went on:

> 'I hereby further declare that the Provisional Executive and the Provisional Army Council are the lawful Executive and Army

Council respectively of the IRA and that the Governmental authority delegated in the Proclamation of 1938 now resides in the Provisional Army Council and its lawful successors.'

The first Provisional IRA's Chief-of-Staff was Ruairí Ó Brádaigh, who soon gave way to Seán MacStiofáin. Many activists from the forties and fifties came in, people like Dave O'Connell, Joe Cahill, Seamus Twomey and JB O'Hagan.

The ferment intensified in the build-up to the Sinn Féin Árd Fheis billed for the Intercontinental Hotel, Dublin on 10–11 January 1970. It would be a public affair and major interest focused on a resolution seeking a constitutional change, the end of the policy of abstentionism. The necessary two-thirds majority failed to materialise. This was immediately followed by a resolution calling for support for the policies of the IRA Army Council, which *ipso facto* included the dropping of abstention. As a non-constitutional motion this only required a simple majority. The ploy, of course, was swiftly spotted and a large group upped and left the meeting. In a pre-planned move they immediately went to a Dublin city venue to form a care-taker executive of a new (Provisional) Sinn Féin. Ruairí Ó Brádaigh was appointed President and remained on the Provisional Army Council. The Provisional IRA now had its civil wing and a new, 'orthodox', Republican movement was reconstituted.

ARMS FROM DUBLIN

Support from the Irish government continued in parallel. In effect, those elements in the Fianna Fáil administration doing the assisting were now helping finance and arm the 'genuine' republicans of the Provisional IRA. For some in senior positions in Dublin this seemed a natural extension

of the policy not to invade the north but to assist nationalists there to defend themselves. Substantial money, channelled through the Belfast Fund for the Relief of Distress,
and limited military training at Fort Dunree Irish Army
Camp in Donegal were provided. But guns were the big
demand and guns were, ostensibly, on the way.

The moves to arm elements in the north led to a vol-
canic political scandal in Dublin during May of 1970.
Taoiseach Jack Lynch sacked two senior Cabinet ministers, Charles Haughey and Neil Blaney, who, with Captain
James Kelly and others, were brought before the Irish
courts charged with conspiracy to import arms illegally. A
District Court found that Blaney had no case to answer.
The others were acquitted in the High Court. The undis-
puted fact was that a large shipment of arms was procured
in Vienna in March–April 1970, but was not sent to Dublin
as planned. John Kelly (not to be confused with Captain
Kelly), a militant Belfast republican, was the link-man in
the proposed transfer of the arms to a monastery in Cavan
for shipment north. The arms were to be taken over by
some ill-defined nationalist 'Defence Committee' representative of the whole of Northern Ireland; but extraordinarily, according to Seán MacStiofáin, the Provisionals'
Chief-of-Staff, they had been destined for his command.
As it happened he doubted that the guns would ever be
handed over to him and the new Provisional Army Council had prepared a plan to hijack the guns and bring them
north.

Those were days of great drama coupled with a fair
degree of political naivety. It would be a year or so before
the full intent and capacity of the 'Provos' became apparent and the old lines between the southern authorities
and the IRA were re-drawn. No-one could have foretold

then that a full quarter of a century of an unremitting, brutal bombing and killing campaign was about to unfold. The new Provisional IRA soon set their sights on 'Victory '72'. Before that they had a major job of organisation, arming and training to contend with. The first task was one of defence.

FROM DEFENCE TO ATTACK, 1972–1976

The years 1970 to 1976 saw another violent see-saw in the fortunes of the Republican movement in the north. At the start of that period, there were two IRAs – 'Officials' and 'Provisionals' – and two Sinn Féins, similarly split. Neither of the rival organisations had a substantial membership or much in the way of arms. The Officials claimed to have held on to 70 percent of its volunteers while the Provisionals became a magnet for many of the younger northern 'sixty-niners', those caught in the maelstrom of the 1969 street violence. Both competed for new recruits and for control of the republican movement at a time when it looked as if any renewed armed campaign would collapse in the face of overwhelming British military force.

Competition and feuding between the two organisations persisted over the years. But in a relatively short time the Provisionals gained dominance. Their appeal was simple and direct – unfettered militarism, no ifs or buts or complicating theories. Their cause, their methods and their recruitment were greatly enhanced by the extraordinarily ham-fisted use of internment in the north in 1971. The subsequent explosion of anger in the nationalist communities propelled the 'Provos', as the Provisional IRA quickly became known, to switch from defensive to offensive action. They reached their military and political peak in

1972, fuelling their ambition to dizzying heights. Final victory over the British, so long dreamed of, planned for, fought for, died for, seemed just around the corner. But just four years later, the Provos were once more facing defeat and yet another period of internal disillusionment and rupture.

GETTING IT GOING

When the movement split in 1969 into the Official and Provisional wings, the Official IRA remained wedded to its strategy of political action through the development of a National Liberation Front and participation in the three parliaments. They had got a clear majority for these policies at the December Convention. Their units in the north were faced with a violent reality. They continued to be strong in Derry, which had become highly politicised through civil rights action. Belfast had been seriously weakened by the disaffiliation of its entire Brigade prior to the split but in pockets the Officials had strong local followings. Whatever about numbers, Goulding's volunteers had the command structure, the contacts and a good deal of military expertise. Their ambitions and their tactics had changed, of course.

Within two years, on 29 May 1972, the (Official) IRA called a ceasefire which became permanent. In between they had killed twenty-five people, including one politician, and had attempted to assassinate Unionist minister John Taylor. They also bombed the HQ of the Parachute Regiment at Aldershot in Hampshire where seven people, including five women canteen workers, died. Then, suddenly, it was over. The Officials were on the road to politics, though its units remained in being for defensive purposes (principally against the Provos) and the Official

IRA as such never disbanded, nor handed in its arms. They might be needed at the final push against the capitalists!

The Provisionals, however, set out their grandiose stall at an early stage. As always their objectives were couched in the quasi-socialist language of taking on imperialist interests, along the lines of the 1916 Proclamation. They sought, not participation in the Stormont Parliament, but its abolition, as an interim measure pending the overturning of the 1920–1922 Treaty arrangements.

In pursuit of that objective the Provisionals killed 15 people in 1970, 89 people in 1971 and 243 people in 1972. It was a concerted and terrifying shooting and bombing campaign designed to force the British government to the negotiating table. Central to this campaign was organisation and resources. A great deal of money flowed in from America in particular, where a Provisional fund-raising organisation was set up called the Irish Northern Aid Committee, known as NORAID. Early attempts to acquire consignments of guns were patchy and often obstructed by successful British intelligence counter-measures. Organisationally, the Provisionals tied up the pivotal zone of Belfast. Unlike the patchy groupings that made up the Officials, a Belfast Brigade with three battalions under its control was put in place with an overall Commanding Officer, Billy McKee.

There was an avowedly non-militaristic nationalist re-alignment too. On 21 August 1970, the Social Democratic and Labour Party (SDLP) was formed under the leadership of Gerry Fitt and including leading civil rights campaigners like John Hume. Once again Irish nationalism divided over the issue of armed force.

That year, 1970, saw another significant political shift with the coming to power at Westminster of the

Conservatives under a new and pragmatic Prime Minister, Edward Heath, a man willing to make bold moves in Northern Ireland. Heath came to the job while the Provisionals were not yet at 'war' with Great Britain. During 1970 the British Army was regarded positively by the nationalists and with suspicion by the loyalists. The Army was generally seen to have come to relieve the embattled nationalists of Belfast and Derry, under assault from rampaging loyalists, and after the collapse of RUC morale. In a strange stand-off alliance the British Army and the Provisional IRA, still in a purely defensive posture, were co-operating against loyalist incursions. In Belfast that changed somewhat after the Falls Road curfew of 3 to 5 July when the Army intensively searched the area, coming away with up to a hundred assorted guns.

But the Provos had yet to turn their guns on the British Army. Serious riots in Ballymurphy, west Belfast, led to a major, heavy Army response, further alienating the locals. In Ballymurphy, a twenty-two year old man by the name of Gerry Adams, who was from a strong militant family tradition, was emerging as the local Provo leader. In February 1971, during disturbances in another Belfast command area, the first British soldier was killed by the Provos. Within a short time Provisional activists were shooting and sniping at soldiers on the streets, across walls, around corners. It was heady, exhilarating stuff for the volunteers and watching spectators, a curious blend of open and guerrilla warfare where the local units could melt back into the housing estates.

THE PROVISIONALS GO ON THE OFFENSIVE

In March 1971, Belfast Brigade came under the command of Joe Cahill, fifty-one year old veteran of the 1940s IRA campaign, who would become a key player in marshalling assistance from the United States. Internment without trial came in August 1971. Hundreds of Catholics were rounded up, and many were beaten and tortured, though they were unconnected and irrelevant to the IRA campaigns, Provisional or Official. Internment became a huge rallying point at home and abroad for the Irish nationalist cause. It was the final signal for the Provisional Army Council to begin a consciously offensive armed insurrection, with the declared objective of driving the British forces out of Northern Ireland.

Internment also provided the Provisionals with powerful propaganda material in their calls for funds, arms and recruits. The urgent task at the time was building an American support and fund-raising network to procure arms. In September 1971, two of the Provos' American-based arms procurers compiled a progress report for MacStiofáin. In the document they wrote of unsuccessfully searching for anti-tank equipment but said 'there had been a total of sixteen successful shipments' to date. The document went on: 'I am happy to report that we expanded our purchase of ammunitions, M1 Gerard rifles, grease guns, pistols and other arms ... the biggest stock we ever had since we started.' These men had been to Ireland for discussions with Seán MacStiofáin, Dave O'Connell, Joe Cahill 'and our three import agents at Dublin'. They were there, in particular, 'to discuss finances for a shipment of arms from Europe'.

New arms contacts were opened up in Europe behind the Iron Curtain. One shipment in late 1971 represented a major breakthrough but also a demoralising failure. Using a complicated web of contacts, a significant consignment of modern weapons including sub-machine guns, bazookas and rifles was bought by Dave O'Connell directly from Omnipol, the Czechoslovakian state arms manufacturer. Then, at the point of departure, the arms consignment was impounded by the Dutch authorities at Schipol Airport on 16 October 1971. It was a major loss of the kind of heavy material being demanded by the northern IRA units. On another level, it showed the Provos buying arms from an Eastern Bloc Communist state while simultaneously appealing for American funds on the basis that the Provisionals were anti-Communist.

FORCING BRITAIN'S HAND

Guns were, of course, a vital ingredient in the IRA's attempts to escalate their campaign and force a British political response. But the major impact was made by explosives used in a myriad of ways: car bombs, nail bombs, the carrier-bag bomb, bombs walked into Belfast city centre by women pretending to be pregnant, cigarette packet incendiary devices. In 1971 the British authorities recovered one ton of explosives, in 1972, eighteen tons. The destruction and the carnage was horrendous and unprecedented, far more powerful than anything done in the 1919–1921 period, concentrated as this was in one corner of the island. But 1972 was the peak. The Provos could never again reach it for its mass effect. Terror was the tactic. The military objective was to create a fortress-like atmosphere where the north could be governed only by military means. This, in turn, would bring the collapse of Northern Ireland as a viable entity, forcing the British government into making radical political changes. From the Provos' point of view the signs and the omens looked good.

The British government had a many-sided problem to

deal with, that went beyond the Provisional IRA. Unionism was in turmoil, with the Unionists feeling betrayed and besieged. Loyalist killing squads had geared up, at times with the assistance of the British Army, who saw the 'loyalists' as useful allies in the fight against the local 'rebels', a tactic employed in former rebellious colonies. In September 1971 the Ulster Defence Association (UDA) was formed, drawing support from loyalist working-class areas of Belfast in particular. For many in those areas the UDA was seen as an unofficial replacement for the B-Specials, their new shield against the IRA. The UDA became a formidable force on the ground, reaching a peak, also in 1972, of about 40,000 members. In that year loyalist groups of varying kinds killed 111 people, mostly ordinary Catholics.

The grim year of 1972 began with 'Bloody Sunday', marked by the shooting dead of thirteen innocent people by the British Parachute Regiment after a civil rights march in Derry. The response in nationalist Ireland was convulsive, greatly strengthening the position of the Provisionals. In March, Ted Heath's government abolished the Stormont Parliament, instigating Direct Rule and placing law and order firmly under British government political and military control. Many factors had brought about this momentous change, not least the Unionists' own intransigence. But for the Provisional Army Council this was success on an epoch-making scale. They were now face-to-face with the British after just sixteen months in existence. Morale was sky-high. On 26 June 1972 the Provos called a halt for a 'bi-lateral truce' and on 7 July, in an astonishing turn of events, the new Northern Ireland Secretary William Whitelaw secretly met the Provisional IRA leadership in London.

The truce and talks had been facilitated by two nationalist politicians, John Hume and Paddy Devlin, acting as intermediaries between the Provisionals and the British. One of the terms the Army Council demanded and got through the intermediaries was 'the immediate release of a senior officer of the Belfast Brigade from internment' for their negotiating team. That person was Gerry Adams. The full team, flown in by RAF helicopter, was MacStiofáin, Chief-of-Staff; Adams; Martin McGuinness, C/O Derry Brigade; Seamus Twomey, Ivor Bell, Dave O'Connell.

There was no pretence of it being a Sinn Féin delegation. These were direct talks with the Provisional IRA leadership. In the end the talks got nowhere. Whitelaw could see that the Provisionals were not in the business of compromise. In any event MacStiofáin was under pressure from some Belfast elements opposed to the truce, men who believed they had the British on the ropes, that this was not the time to lift the pressure. There were suspicions that some of these activists in Belfast helped engineer a breakdown of the truce. It ended on 10 July in a hostile atmosphere of mutual recrimination, the ostensible breaking-point being street clashes with British troops in Lenadoon, west Belfast. Whitelaw had already read the Provisionals' demands into the record of the House of Commons. These were:

1. A public declaration by the British Government that it is the right of all the people of Ireland acting as a unit to decide the future of Ireland.

2. A declaration of intent to withdraw British forces from Irish soil by 1 January 1975. Pending this, the immediate withdrawal of British forces from sensitive areas.

3. A general amnesty for all political prisoners in both countries, for internees and detainees, and for persons on the wanted list.

However it was explained, these talks had the look of the British government 'recognising' the Provisional Army Council as a body to negotiate the future of Ireland. In Dublin, Taoiseach Jack Lynch said as much in a severe public criticism of the British. The encounter massively encouraged MacStiofáin's men, giving them the belief in ultimate success which had eluded all other IRA leaderships. MacStiofáin's response to the talks failure was to 'escalate, escalate and escalate' until the British conceded the demands. That July was the worst month in the entire northern troubles – 200 explosions, 95 dead, 2,800 shooting incidents. Whitelaw was caught out and vowed never again to hold secret talks with the IRA. The combination of those two responses ensured that the Provisionals' campaign would continue indefinitely.

The old hands like MacStiofáin, Twomey, Cahill and O'Connell firmly believed that events would propel the IRA and Sinn Féin into power, in a repeat of the 1918 tidal wave, and that, with the northern parliament abolished, Dáil Éireann would follow. Finally the all-Ireland republic would be re-established. In their scheme of things this would be a federal state, comprising four subordinate provincial regional parliaments with a Federal government in the central location of Athlone. It was very much the brainchild of Ruairí Ó Brádaigh and Dave O'Connell. Called 'Éire Nua' (New Ireland), the proposal was a significant deviation from the classic Irish republican unitary state model. For that reason it was to have huge significance in a later internal power struggle.

THE ROAD TO DEMORALISATION

While 1972 was the year of Seán MacStiofáin's peak performance it was also the year of his eclipse. In November he was arrested in Dublin, charged with IRA membership under emergency laws and immediately went on hunger-strike. After some high-noon drama of an attempted rescue from a Dublin hospital, MacStiofáin was given a six months' gaol sentence but also broke his hunger-strike. It was a very public humiliation for the toughest of the toughest Chief-of-Staff. MacStiofáin never recovered his rank and faded away, to be replaced by Joe Cahill and then Seamus Twomey.

The following year, 1973, began with the Provisionals pledging that the struggle would go on, that more casualties would be inflicted until the British government 'recognises that policies which failed in Cyprus, Aden and Palestine will also fail in Ireland'. The New Year statement also declared that the granting of the Éire Nua peace proposals would result in a 'suspension of offensive military action on the part of the IRA'. The offensive continued unabated. In May 1973 Joe Cahill was taken out of the scene when he got five years for gun-running on the ship, the *Claudia*, seized off the Waterford coast with a large arms consignment from Libya.

Those were days of great uncertainty. With no locally elected administration a dangerous political vacuum existed in the north. Then the British government made a bold move. Ignoring the two extremes of loyalism and republicanism, William Whitelaw sought to build on a solid centre. In December, at Sunningdale in England, a full-scale conference took place involving the two governments and the northern constitutional parties. Out of it came an agreement which stunned hardline unionism and left Irish nationalism believing that a huge historical leap forward had taken place. The Sunningdale Agreement set up a power-sharing administration and

Assembly in Belfast, comprising moderate Unionism led by Brian Faulkner, moderate nationalism in the form of the SDLP and a new cross-community group, the Alliance Party.

It was historic in its dimensions, the biggest British move on the Irish question since the Treaty. The centre-piece for nationalists was a Council of Ireland, a free-standing Irish body comprising seven ministers each from the new Assembly and the Irish government. Alongside this would be an advisory body of sixty elected representatives, thirty from each parliament north and south. On the issue of Irish unity a significant and enduring benchmark was laid down in the Agreement. The Irish government accepted that there could be no change in the status of Northern Ireland until a majority of its people desired it. For its part, the British government pledged to support the wish of a majority in Northern Ireland for Irish unity should such be forthcoming.

The Provisionals' response was to reject the Sunningdale Agreement, on the grounds that it copper-fastened British rule and Partition. They would fight on, for the next twenty years as it happened, killing and bombing for an outright British withdrawal, not to be attained in those twenty years of violence. No Irish or British government sought it nor would grant it over the heads of the northern Unionists. The old stumbling block of the north which stymied the Treaty negotiators back in 1921 was still an immovable obstacle. But this new generation of IRA leaders still sniffed final victory. The 1972 talks with Whitelaw had set the scent. To a point they would be proven right. The British did talk to them again. It wasn't victory they got but virtual defeat.

For now, in 1974, the new power-sharing administration

was up and running. If it lasted it would pose a serious threat to the Provisionals' capacity to hold any significant measure of nationalist support. That was why they were intent on destroying it, as they were with any compromise settlement short of their final goal. The power-sharing administration *was* brought down, but principally by the fury of the hardline Unionists. Paisleyism, loyalist paramilitarism and senior Unionist figures combined against it. For them, Sunningdale was a bridge too far, a sure pathway to a united Ireland. Moderate unionism failed to hold the centre ground.

In May 1974 the fledgling power-sharing administration at Stormont collapsed in the face of a massive loyalist workers' strike, strengthened by the inaction of the British security forces. Harold Wilson, back in power in London, let the arrangements die. With it went the Council of Ireland. Nationalists in the north faced into years of isolation from the south and aggressive posturing from a triumphalist Unionist camp, including lethal loyalist assassination campaigns. In this atmosphere the Provisionals were well able to justify their existence as the army of a beleaguered people.

HOPE AND TERROR

Defending their people was not the Provos' primary objective. Had it been so their killing rate would have been low. They remained on the offensive, trying to force a British withdrawal. Their killings remained relentlessly high – 140 in 1974 as 'Victory '74' became a belief and a slogan. The year ended with a mixture of terror and hope. On 21 November 1974, twenty-one people died in two pub bombings in Birmingham. The shock and outrage was enormous. The 'Birmingham Six' who were imprisoned for the murders, eventually won acquittal and release more than sixteen years later. It was years before the Provisionals admitted to the Birmingham bombs. At the time, in an exceptionally speedy response, the British Labour government rushed through extra tough emergency legislation, the Prevention of Terrorism Act.

It was in that highly charged atmosphere, with the Irish community in Britain backed against the wall and anti-Provo sentiment surging across Ireland, that hope appeared. Through the intervention of senior Protestant clergymen an extended Christmas unilateral ceasefire was followed by a seven-month agreed truce, beginning on 10 February 1975. Against all the odds, the way had been opened again for direct talks between the Provisional IRA and the British government. This time, British ministers stayed safely out of it. Their negotiators were senior civil servants, including Frank Cooper of the Northern Ireland Office and James Alan from the Foreign Office. Ruairí Ó Brádaigh and Billy McKee led for the Provisionals.

What happened next has remained etched in the memory of the Republican movement as one of the bitterest and most debilitating episodes in its recent history. At its heart was the *purpose* of the negotiations. Ó Brádaigh insisted that, during the Christmas ceasefire, the Provisionals' leadership received a message from the British stating that 'HMG wished to devise structures of disengagement from Ireland'. The word 'disengagement' could only mean a complete British pull-out. The British side have denied this. Their view was that, if the talks succeeded, they could have resulted in a complete withdrawal of British troops from internal security: a significant move, but not in the same league as 'disengagement'. The British did give a *verbal* commitment that the purpose of the talks was 'to

89

bring about withdrawal from Ireland', without doubt an ambiguous phrase open to Ó Brádaigh's interpretation.

In retrospect, it is clear that the British never seriously contemplated disengagement but rather used the long-drawn-out negotiations to pull the Provisionals towards compromise and into politics. Specifically, the British hoped that (Provisional) Sinn Féin would agree to enter the elected Constitutional Convention, designed to get an agreed government for Northern Ireland. The election was set for 1 May 1975 at a time when the talks were going strong. In the end Sinn Féin stayed out, as they had stayed out of all elections to that point. The British belief was that Ó Brádaigh's side *was* ready to settle for a compromise (withdrawal of the British army to Britain and an amnesty for prisoners) but that they got into difficulties with leading 'hard men' coming out of the prisons. Certainly, the activists on the outside were getting edgy, wondering if it was all a British ploy and watching the loyalists continue with assassinations. The truce simply petered out, ending on 22 September 1975.

By the end, the IRA was seriously demoralised, badly infiltrated and considerably weakened. They could well have split, splintered or shut up shop at that time. Worst of all, from their viewpoint, the British government had used the long truce to upgrade their administration of Northern Ireland, in particular ending political status for prisoners and giving control of security to the Royal Ulster Constabulary: ie, a policy of 'normalisation, Ulsterisation and criminalisation'.

Through 1976 the Provisionals continued with ferocity but also great uncertainty. The 'hard men' were set against any form of temporary stoppage. Yet the political door was firmly shut. When Roy Mason became Secretary of State for Northern Ireland in September 1976 there followed the harshest of regimes against the Provos, a strategy of hunt and defeat. By the Provisionals' own admission it was a strategy that worked.

THE LONG WAR, 1976–1980

> The three-day and seven-day detention orders are breaking volunteers and it is the Republican Army's fault for not indoctrinating volunteers with the psychological strength to resist interrogation.
>
> Coupled with this factor, which is contributing to our defeat, we are burdened with an inefficient infrastructure of commands, Brigades, Battalions and Companies. This old system, with which the Brits and Branch are familiar, has to be changed. We recommend reorganisation and remotivation, the building of a new Irish Republican Army.

That was the opening statement from an IRA Staff Report in 1977. It represented a clear admission of failure by the leadership. They would have to start again. They did start again and in the forefront of the renewal was a coterie of 'hard men' in the north gathered around Gerry Adams and Martin McGuinness. They were backed in HQ by Chief-of-Staff Seamus Twomey.

From the north Adams and McGuinness had led the oblique criticism of the Ó Bradaigh–O'Connell axis based in Dublin. Writing from 'The Kesh' prison, Adams had penned a semi-regular column in *Republican News* under the name 'Brownie'. Brownie's constant theme was the politicisation of the struggle, how to fight a long war without becoming isolated from the people. Gone were the heady themes of 'Victory '72' or 'Victory '74'. It would have to be a long war or yet another inglorious ending, the 'dumping' of guns for another generation. To fight a long war there would have to be a great break with tradition. Dublin could no longer run the campaign as it had done on all previous occasions since the 1920s.

THE NORTHERNERS TAKE CONTROL

Adams and McGuinness operated in the 'War Zone'. Dublin had led them into the *cul de sac* of the debilitating long truce. There must now be a Northern Command. In late 1976 the northerners, Adams and McGuinness and Ivor Bell, backed by Twomey, got their way. A Northern Command was established. It would run the 'War Zone', comprising the six counties of Northern Ireland plus the five adjoining southern Border counties. Southern Command, encompassing the other twenty-one counties, would effectively become quartermaster to Northern Command, its supplier of materials. The centre of gravity had, inevitably, shifted north. The Adams camp was taking control.

Coupled with this came the complete revamping of the IRA as set out in the Staff Report. Gone would be the looser, flabbier structure which was well infiltrated and where undisciplined volunteers were prey to interrogation. Now there would be a tighter, leaner, fitter, smaller cell structure; what the Staff Report called a new Irish Republican Army. 'We must gear ourselves towards long--term armed struggle based on putting unknown men and new recruits into a new structure.' The cells, mostly of four activists, would apply mainly to town and city areas where there had been too much loose talk. Secrecy and speciali-sation would be the watchword. 'Cells must be specialised into IO (intelligence) cells, sniping cells, executions, bombings, robberies, etc.'

Underlining the need for a complete overhaul of the Republican movement, military and non-military, control by the IRA would be essential. 'Army men must be in total control of all sections of the movement,' the Staff Report said bluntly. Cumann na mBan (the women's republican support group founded back in 1913) would be dissolved 'with the best being incorporated in IRA cell structure'. The youth wing, Na Fianna Éireann (founded in 1909 as a recruiting ground for the Irish Republican Brotherhood) would 'return to being an underground organisation ... they should be educated and organised decisively to pass into IRA cell structure when of age.'

The Report also spelt out a new role for Sinn Féin, once more re-enforcing the 'supreme authority' of the IRA Army Council. Sinn Féin, it said, should be 'radicalised (under Army direction) and should agitate around social and economic issues ... should be directed to infiltrate other organisations to win support for, and sympathy to, the Movement.' Radicalising Sinn Féin meant a shift left-wards and a shift to politics.

On the surface there was a semblance of *déjà vu* about this 'radicalisleing' programme, a touch of what Cathal Goulding's people attempted in the 1960s and which continued apace. At exactly the time the Provisionals were gearing up for a long war strategy the Officials made one more shift to politics. In January 1977 (Official) Sinn Féin changed its name to 'Sinn Féin the Workers Party', signalling its deepening involvement in electoral politics from an avowedly hard left position. The Official IRA ceasefire of 1972 still held, though the guns were taken out a number of times to settle old scores, in particular to combat a new paramilitary group, the Irish National Liberation Army, which had split off from the Officials in 1975. Official IRA guns were also used for robberies and to enforce protection rackets in the north. But 'armed strugg' against the

British was over for the Officials.

In sharp contrast the Provisionals' armed struggle would be upgraded rather than downgraded. Politics would not be a *substitute* for armed action, as Goulding had it, but rather an essential support base for it. Unlike the Officials, Adams and McGuinness *et al* would continue the fight to force Britain out of Ireland. But they would also try to radicalise and broaden the struggle. Instead of the IRA being isolated and defeated, they would win mass support for the armed struggle, based on a politicised anti-imperialist programme tightly controlled by the IRA leadership.

The restructuring of the Republican movement had another inevitable consequence, the removal of the Ó Brádaigh–O'Connell leadership. That leadership was held responsible, with varying degrees of venom, for the long truce and the near defeat of the IRA. The change took time, from 1977 to 1983, and the tactic used was not a direct attack on the leadership. It was the undermining of Ó Brádaigh and O'Connell's most vaunted political policy, 'Éire Nua', the proposal for a Federal Ireland.

Internally the Adams–McGuinness group was expanding. It took in Danny Morrison the chief publicist, and a number of other Belfast political strategists like Tom Hartley and got the name of the 'Falls Road think-tank'. They took control of the *Republican News*, based in Belfast, which they then amalgamated with *An Phoblacht*, published from HQ in Dublin. This gave the northerners control of the Republican movement's national publication, which was profoundly influential within that kind of secretive, conspiratorial organisation. Sympathetic prisoners were also involved, conveniently getting their views aired in *An Phoblacht*.

Together, these people pressed for a return to the traditional uncompromising goal of a unitary Irish state. They won the debate and won the day. In 1981, Sinn Féin dropped the 'Éire Nua' policy, fatally undermining the existing leadership. Then, unexpectedly, came a tumult in the north which further accelerated the change. The long hunger-strikes of 1981, when ten republican prisoners including Bobby Sands died in the Maze Prison, led to political and community convulsions north of the Border. Media attention on an enormous scale further raised the profiles of the northerners, especially when Bobby Sands got elected on an abstentionist ticket to Westminster for Fermanagh–South Tyrone.

Ó Brádaigh himself had long since been excluded from Northern Ireland by law and had to content himself with media isolation in the south. There, the IRA, Sinn Féin and other such groups were banned from the national airwaves by Ministerial Directive. Then in 1983 the inevitable happened. The northern bandwagon couldn't be stopped.

Sinn Féin had notched up an astonishing 102,000 votes in the Westminster general election of June 1983. Adams himself made worldwide news by getting elected in west Belfast. Overtaking the main nationalist party, the SDLP now led by John Hume, was a prize ripe for grasping. Triumph and high ambition were in the air again, just like the early 1970s. At the Sinn Féin Árd Fheis in November 1983, Gerry Adams was elected President. The baton had passed on. It was passed to the 'sixty-niners', that group of toughened activists, born out of the northern conflagrations of 1969 rather than from the Holy Grail theology of 1919. Their brash pragmatism would make its mark down the line. Gerry Adams and his group were in control, at the highest levels of the IRA and its civil wing, Sinn Féin.

At the Árd Fheis Adams made no bones about welding together the military and the political in the public mind. In his first speech as President, Adams addressed the issue of armed struggle head on:

> 'Armed struggle is a necessary and morally correct form of resistance in the Six Counties against a government whose presence is rejected by the vast majority of the Irish people.'

The sustained applause in Dublin's Mansion House rose to new heights when Adams went on:

> 'There are those who tell us that the British Government will not be moved by armed struggle. As has been said before, the history of Ireland and of British colonial involvement throughout the world tells us that they will not be moved by anything else.'

By that stage the long war had been in progress for six years. The killings continued but the revamped RUC was making its mark too. From a high point in killings, (243) in 1972, the IRA killed 70 in 1977; 56 in 1978; 93 in 1979; 45 in 1980; 59 in 1981; 52 in 1982 and 50 in 1983. The leaner, fitter IRA had well and truly survived. Through significant political advances in republican heartlands they had made it impossible to be isolated and defeated. The long war strategy was working. Yet there was no end in sight, no sign of victory. British rule in Northern Ireland was deep, stabilised and secure. The IRA was facing the toughest of British prime ministers, Margaret Thatcher. The task of forcing a British withdrawal was getting harder not easier.

THE GREEN BOOK

Once the IRA geared up for a long war strategy they needed to instill strong belief and commitment into the volunteers. This would not be like the frenetic early days and months,

Above: The aftermath of the 1916 Easter Rising: British forces hold a Dublin street against the insurgents.

Above: Two Republican prisoners from Enniscorthy, Co Wexford, being escorted to Kilmainham Gaol, Dublin, under heavy guard and accompanied by a British army officer and RIC sergeant in 1916.

Above: A group of Sinn Féin leaders, wanted by the British government, relax at a hurling match in Croke Park, Dublin, 1921.
Front row, left to right: Arthur Griffith, Eamon de Valera, Laurence O'Neill (Lord Mayor of Dublin) and Michael Collins.

Above: A group of British Auxiliary Cadets, known as the 'Black and Tans', outside their headquarters at Union Quay, Cork, in 1921.

Above: Prisoners rounded up by British troops and 'Black and Tans' after the Custom House battle in 1921.

Right: Sounding the alarm – a whistle used to alert members of West Limerick IRA of advancing British forces, 1921.

Above: Changing of the Guard – British army troops leave as Irish Free State troops arrive, Dublin, 1922.

Left: Cumann na nGael election poster, general election 1927.

Left: One-time IRA Chief-of-Staff Seán MacStiofáin faded from the republican scene after his arrest for IRA membership in 1972.

Below: IRA volunteers fire the traditional volley of shots over the body of Bobby Sands, who died on 5 May 1981 after sixty-six days on hunger-strike in the Maze prison.

Above: Masked petrol-bombers in nationalist Bogside Derry
after the Protestant Apprentice Boys March, 1986.

Above: Ruairí Ó Brádaigh leaves the Sinn Féin Árd Fheis to found
Republican Sinn Féin, 1986.

Above: Provisional IRA (1990s) demonstrating AK-47 Kalashnikov rifles, which were part of Libyan arms shipments from the 1980s.

Above: An IRA bomb at the Baltic Exchange in London, on 10 April 1992, killed three people and left a compensation bill of stg£600 million.

Left: 28 July 2005 IRA campaign ends. Former IRA activist Seanna Walsh reads statement: 'The Leadership of Óglaigh na hÉireann has formally ordered an end to the armed campaign. This will take effect from 4.00pm this afternoon.'

Below: 26 March 2007: DUP Leader Ian Paisley and Sinn Féin President Gerry Adams announce agreement to enter a power-sharing Executive on 8 May 2007.

filled with excitement, history-making, even romanticism. A new training manual for the new IRA known as the Green Book, was drawn up. New recruits were 'green booked', educated in its contents, told the cold realities of killing. Volunteers were also told they had 'moral superiority'. They were instructed that the IRA's leadership was the lawful government of the Irish Republic and that this gave them the moral justification to use force:

> Volunteers must firmly believe without doubt and without reservation that, as members of the Irish Republican Army, all orders issued by the Army Authority and all actions directed by the Army Authority are the legal orders and the lawful actions of the Government of the Irish Republic. This is one of the most important mainstays of the Republican Movement.

It was a message pressed home strongly, when it came to training the recruit to kill:

> ... before any potential volunteer decides to join the Army he must have these strong convictions. Convictions which are strong enough to give him confidence to kill someone without hesitation and without regret.

The strategy was to build a politicised fighting force, with a clear radical objective:

> ... the actions of the Army are directed towards a political objective. That is the real meaning of the present military campaign. The Army as a political force are intent on creating a socialist Republic in this country, therefore all potential volunteers must be socialist in outlook.

The long-term objective was described as the Democratic Socialist Republic: short-term objectives being 'hurdles or obstacles which must be cleared from our path' on the

97

road to that goal. 'The Brits out campaign is therefore our national short-term objective.'

The targets of that campaign were spelt out, the enemies categorised into those who should be 'executed' and those who could be ridiculed or exposed as liars, hypocrites and collaborators. The overall guerrilla strategy, designed to effect a British withdrawal, was outlined in five points:

1. A war of attrition against enemy personnel which is aimed at causing as many casualties and deaths as possible, so as to create a demand from their people at home for withdrawal.

2. A bombing campaign aimed at making the enemy's financial interest in our country unprofitable while at the same time curbing long-term investment in our country.

3. To make the Six Counties as at present and for the past several years ungovernable except by colonial military rule.

4. To sustain the war and gain support for its ends by national and international propaganda and publicity campaigns.

5. Defending the war of liberation by punishing criminals, collaborators and informers.

This was a strategy calculated to inflict death and destruction for as long as it took to achieve the stated short-term objective and build a platform for the final goal:

By now it is clear that our task is not only to kill as many enemy personnel as possible or to cause as much economic damage as possible but of equal importance to create support which will carry us not only through a war of liberation which could last another decade but which will support us past the 'Brits out' stage to the ultimate aim of a Democratic Socialist Republic.

Along the way they would prevent their isolation by 'IRA

involvement with all anti-imperialist groupings' and by channelling nationalist resentment into a form of resistance against the British presence. Resistance in turn would be channelled into active and passive support for the Republican movement and the IRA's campaign. The alternative would lead to isolation and defeat:

> If, for example, we have an area with a unit of IRA volunteers and nothing else: no Sinn Féin Cumann, no Green Cross committee [for fund raising], no local involvement, etc. After a period, regardless of how successfully [sic] they have been against the Brits, they end up in jail leaving no structures behind: no potential for resistance, recruits, education or general enhancing of support.

This attempt to politicise and radicalise the IRA and to radicalise Sinn Féin was now in the hands of the new leadership. It led to extensive education programmes within the prisons, within Sinn Féin and the wider communities. Volunteers and supporters were instructed that the main historical obstacle to the Republic, the Unionists of the north, should only be viewed as Britain's 'junior partner': their proclaimed Britishness was bogus and carried no merit. Among a series of published lectures for its members, Sinn Féin addressed the issue of loyalism, dismissing its claim to a separate heritage as a 'myth'. The Sinn Féin lecture concluded by saying that 'loyalism is an ideology and politics that can in no way be compromised with, short of the achievement of a united Ireland'. The short-term objective of 'Brits out' would be clear, untainted and without deviation.

The twin-track strategy, encapsulated in the IRA's Green Book, backed up by the Sinn Féin lecture series governed the Republican movement's armed actions and their political tactics from the late 1970s, through the 1980s and into the 1990s. At first, momentum was impressive and success considerable. The IRA prevented isolation and remained undefeated. But, as the long war progressed, it became clear that the overall strategy was a failure.

THE HUMAN COST

Nowhere in the Green Book did the IRA leadership place a limit on the number of casualties or the amount of destruction. They knew they faced into a decade or more of military action. Therefore, appeals for them to stop were, in effect, dismissed in advance. Inevitably that had been their response to Pope John Paul's plea 'on my bended knees', during his visit to Ireland in September 1979. A month earlier the IRA had showed their intentions with two of their most significant strikes on the one day, 27 August. They killed eighteen British soldiers in explosions at Warrenpoint, Co Down. It was the British Army's biggest single-incident loss of the conflict. That same day at Mullaghmore, Co Sligo, came one of the IRA's most high-profile assaults when, in a radio-triggered explosion, a boat carrying Lord Mountbatten of Burma, a member of the British royal family, was blown to pieces. Lord Mountbatten died instantly as did his fourteen year old grandson and another fourteen year old boy crewing the boat. The new British Prime Minister, Margaret Thatcher, responded by tightening security.

Politically, the cards were falling right for the IRA, encouraging them to persist. In Dublin Charles Haughey came to the leadership of Fianna Fáil and the office of Taoiseach in December 1979. Haughey had recovered from the Arms Trial debacle of 1970 and clearly won the support of the strong republican side of his party. As

Taoiseach he made it clear that the north was his top priority and that he favoured a British withdrawal. A year later, Haughey and Thatcher made what the new Taoiseach called 'a historic breakthrough' at a summit in Dublin. A programme of joint studies by the two governments was instigated covering a wide range of issues within the island of Ireland. The high-powered meeting, where Thatcher was accompanied by her Foreign Secretary, Lord Carrington, and Chancellor of the Exchequer, Sir Geoffrey Howe, agreed to proceed on the basis of the 'totality of relationships' between the two islands. It had the whiff of constitutional change about it and Dublin more than hinted that a united Ireland had come a step closer.

None of this was to suggest that Haughey was encouraging the IRA. But these political moves led the Republican movement's leadership to believe that Haughey would deliver real change, in particular that he would not settle for a purely internal solution to the conflict in Northern Ireland. They would continue with their campaign of killing, wounding and destruction, the vital cutting edge for change. One way or another, there was a great deal of new-found optimism within IRA ranks as the 1980s began. They had a leadership from the 'war zone' which, in turn, had a long war strategy already reaching heights and strengths unmatched by anything since the 1920s.

FIGHTING TO A STALEMATE, 1980–1990

Committed as it was to its military and political strategy, the Republican movement found itself unable to reach beyond a certain level of success. Yet for some considerable time its leaders continued to state their belief in final victory. They had reason to hold this belief. Sinn Féin looked set to become the dominant nationalist political force in Northern Ireland. This would roll over into the Republic south of the Border. Gerry Adams was ready and willing to outfox his political opponents in Dublin by changing tack on the hallowed policy of abstention and making a direct pitch for Dáil seats, on a platform of support for the 'war of liberation' in the north. Sinn Féin could even contemplate holding the balance of power in Dáil Éireann, becoming king-makers and government brokers.

As the 1980s progressed, however, the biggest push would come from the IRA on the military front. They showed deadly intent near the start of the decade when, on 14 November 1981, a five-man IRA unit assassinated Rev Robert Bradford, the Ulster Unionist MP for South Belfast. The IRA had bigger ambitions still. The Army Council's secret plans to re-arm and re-equip on a mighty scale, courtesy of Col Ghadaffi in Libya, would ensure a triumphant last heave against the British. This leadership was strong, confident, enduring and pragmatic. Yet Gerry Adams, Martin McGuinness, Chief-of-Staff Kevin McKenna *et al* miscalculated the strength of their opponents. The final push, when it came, fizzled out to a stalemate.

CONTAINMENT

By the start of the 1980s, the British security and intelligence services were making inroads into IRA supplies and morale. The result was a significant squeeze on IRA operations, in particular on their bank robbery activities in the south and on their cross-border logistical activities. There was a certain stretching of the law in these changes, especially within the RUCs Echo 4 Alpha units, made up partly of SAS operatives, specially inducted into the police and co-ordinated with MI5, the British Secret Service.

Some of these special units engaged in high-risk killing missions, responding directly to IRA killings. As always, this opened up propaganda opportunities for the Republican movement which they exploited, in line with their long war strategy of expanding their base of resistance. 'Shoot--to-kill' allegations followed six suspect killings by the RUC units in Co Armagh during 1982, leading to a controversial inquiry by John Stalker, Deputy Chief Constable of the Manchester police. Throughout the conflict, as with the Stalker episode, the use of lethal force by the British Army and RUC was highly contentious.

Under the 1967 Criminal Law (Northern Ireland) Act soldiers and policemen could use force that was 'reasonable in the circumstances'. It was an extremely imprecise legal framework governing 'official' killings and meant that state defence lawyers won acquittal after acquittal where soldiers or police had killed unarmed people. Between 1970 and 1985 British security personnel killed more than 300 people, many of them in circumstances which remained controversial. A number of the victims were children killed by plastic bullets. These disputed killings greatly magnified the hurt felt by people in hard-pressed nationalist areas, especially as their alienation from the state was already a significant factor in the conflict. The British government refused to use the much higher legal standard laid down in Article 2(2) of the European Convention on Human Rights, namely that lethal force could be justified only in cases of 'absolute necessity'. But having decided on a normalisation and criminalisation policy, the British government was determined not to be pushed back to a military regime – one of the IRA's principal objectives – and continued to operate within the law, albeit at times a warped version.

So, within this broad legal framework, the British

authorities kept up the pressure. Between 1981 and 1986 a 'supergrass' system for terrorist-type trials wrought havoc inside the IRA and other paramilitary organisations. The system ended in disrepute, especially when 'supergrasses' withdrew their evidence and trials collapsed. Nonetheless the system provided a massive trawl of intelligence. In its first three years, evidence from about thirty informers led to charges against about 300 people. All of this bred immense dissension within IRA (and other) ranks. Operations had to be stalled while internal inquiries and adjustments were carried out. At the same time these 'show trials', as they were dubbed, also yielded propaganda advantage for the Republican movement.

POLITICAL CONTAINMENT

The most significant containment exercise came in the form of a joint British–Irish political initiative, the most important political advance since the collapse of the Sunningdale Agreement a decade earlier. It arrived in November 1985, a deal struck between Margaret Thatcher and Dr Garret FitzGerald, Taoiseach of the new Fine Gael/Labour coalition government in Dublin. With the very real threat of Sinn Féin political dominance in the north, Dr FitzGerald's government was anxious to curtail the growing alienation of the northern nationalists.

The London–Dublin negotiations were protracted and difficult, stretching out over 1984 and 1985. Though they were highly secret, it was clear that a significant political agreement was in the offing, the kind which would inevitably fall short of the IRA's objective of British withdrawal. As always with a compromise, the IRA sought to destroy it. The IRA claimed to have used more explosives in 1985 than in any other year of the conflict. But they were up against the tenacity of Margaret Thatcher.

The British Prime Minister had narrowly avoided death on 12 October 1984, during the Conservative Party's annual conference in Brighton. A delayed-action IRA bomb partly demolished her hotel while she was asleep. It killed five people, but no minister and not the Prime Minister. The assassination attempt was a huge security breach and a massive boost to IRA morale. Thatcher had become the hate figure ever since she faced down the republican hunger-strikers in 1981. A tactical success, the Brighton bomb could also be described as a strategic failure. It ensured that this British Prime Minister would not yield to the IRA and hers turned out to be a very long prime ministerial tenure.

At the time, the IRA were concerned with the immediate threat. They mounted a sustained assault on the British–Irish political initiative. During May, June and July of 1985 their active service units placed huge bombs, three of 1,000lbs and one of 1,800lbs, in various northern locations. In the process they killed four policemen, destroyed the commercial centre of Ballynahinch, Co Down, demolished part of Belfast's city centre, and blew up the Recorder's Court in Belfast. Plans to launch a seafront bombing campaign in southern Britain were forestalled when bomb-making equipment was discovered in Amsterdam en route to England. In Northern Ireland sustained and widespread attacks were carried out during the autumn of 1985 on RUC stations, army bases, whatever targets could be identified, using 50lb bombs from newly created single-tube mortars.

None of this prevented London and Dublin from finalising negotiations. The IRA offensive was at too low a level to preoccupy Westminster. The 'Ulsterisation' policy of putting the RUC in charge of security made it difficult to get at the British Army, the chief 'forces of occupation'. It meant the IRA's killing missions were failing to hit enough British soldiers and thereby failing 'to create a demand from their people at home for their withdrawal', as the strategy had it. Compared with the heady days of 1972, when 103 soldiers were killed, the coffins going back home to Britain had slowed to a trickle, barely noticed at Westminster: 5 soldiers killed in 1983; with 9 in 1984; 2 in 1985. It was not so much that the IRA could be ignored. But they were unable to inflict their agenda on the political process underway.

On 15 November 1985 the Anglo–Irish Agreement was signed by Thatcher and FitzGerald at Hillsborough Castle, Co Down. Mrs Thatcher had simply swept aside any notion of making moves towards an independent Ireland or towards the exercise of Irish national self-determination. The Agreement also fell far short of Dr FitzGerald's proposal for joint authority by London and Dublin over Northern Ireland. But, for the first time, it gave the Irish government, on behalf of the nationalists, a 'say' in the affairs of Northern Ireland. A joint British–Irish civil service secretariat was established in Belfast. It would act as a channel for complaints and proposals and would service an Inter-Governmental Conference of Ministers which would meet regularly. Article One of the Agreement further reinforced Britain's commitment to legislate for a change in the status of Northern Ireland should a majority there so wish.

Gerry Adams immediately denounced the Agreement, saying it copper-fastened partition. The fact was, however, that the Anglo–Irish Agreement was broadly popular with nationalists. It significantly undermined the Sinn Féin political advance and enhanced the standing of John Hume's SDLP. This was immediately brought home when, in by-elections of January 1986 following resignations by protesting Unionist MPs, Seamus Mallon won a seat in Armagh for the SDLP, easily defeating his Sinn Féin rival. More than anything, there was an ominous warning in this for the IRA's long war strategy. That strategy was constructed on the basis of attacking British rule. Here was a new and more complex enemy. The Anglo–Irish Agreement was a coming together of the British and Irish governments, in a situation where Dublin was given a role representing the grievances and aspirations of the northern nationalists. The London–Dublin axis would deepen over the ensuing years and prove to be a significant obstacle to the IRA's higher ambitions. However, in 1985, there remained the possibility that an incoming Fianna Fáil administration under Charles Haughey would reject the Anglo–Irish Agreement, as Haughey had appeared to do on the night of its publication.

In any event the IRA had its own agenda which it was determined to pursue. They knew that they had been seriously contained on a number of fronts. Yet the leadership's confidence remained high. They had good reason to expect that within a short period they would have the tools to escalate the armed campaign and shorten the long war. During 1985 and 1986 the Republican movement was gearing up for a significant military and political shift of gear.

THE LIBYAN ARMS

The IRA's Libyan route had been re-opened for a number of years, probably since back in 1981 during the hunger-strikes period. Col Ghadaffi had been threatening to support anti-imperialist groups, including the IRA. His regime had come in for sustained attack and criticism from the Anglo–American duo of Margaret Thatcher and US President, Ronald Reagan. A new low in British–Libyan relations was reached in April 1984 when a British police constable, Yvonne Fletcher, was shot dead at the Libyan Embassy in London, leading to the expulsion from Britain of Ghadaffi's diplomatic representatives. Two years later, in April 1986, Reagan and Thatcher combined to launch no-warning air strikes on Tripoli and Benghazi from British military bases. All the while, the IRA was going through an exhaustive process of securing arms from the Libyan regime. Ghadaffi was delivering on his threats.

When the shipments came, they represented the greatest boost to the IRA arsenal in its entire history. The shipments also revealed an international intelligence lapse of mammoth proportions. Coming from Libya via Malta and using the Wicklow coast as a landing spot, about seven tons of arms were brought ashore in August 1985; a further 10 tons in October 1985; 14 tons in July 1986 and, the largest shipment, 105 tons in October 1986. It amounted to a massive haul, enough to sustain the long war for up to twenty more years. The shipments contained 40 general purpose machine guns; 1,200 Kalashnikov semi-automatic assault rifles; 130 Webley revolvers; 50 pistols; 750 detonators; perhaps a million rounds of ammunition. But most importantly for the IRA leadership they had been given the equipment to intensify and escalate the armed assault against the British: about five tons of powerful Semtex commercial explosives; 26 huge DSHK armour-piercing Russian machine guns and ample ammunition to match; 130 RPG rocket launchers; 10 surface-to-air missiles. All of this came free gratis, plus cash estimated at £2million. It was staggering and unbelievable.

Part of the deal with Ghadaffi was that none of the equipment would be used until all the shipments were in. And a fifth shipment was due. This time disaster struck. The ship, the *Eksund*, was seized off the French coast in October 1987. It was carrying 120 tons of arms, almost as much as all of the earlier four shipments combined. The disaster was not so much the loss of equipment. The IRA was well-supplied with the successful loads, which by that stage had been hidden in bunkers, principally in the Munster area. The *Eksund* seizure alerted the British and Irish authorities to the contents of the first four shipments and led to a massive countrywide search of suspect houses and locations south of the Border. In those searches a great deal of disruption was caused to IRA activities and many arms and some significant bunkers were uncovered. North of the Border and in London the British authorities were now forewarned about the coming assault and knew precisely the new weaponry in IRA hands. Still, the IRA *had* the gear, especially the Semtex explosives. Overall, the Libyan haul was a triumph for the IRA and an astounding boost to its ambitions. In a parallel exercise the political tools to achieve those ambitions were being re-shaped.

ABANDONING THE HOLY GRAIL

In many ways the Republican movement was locked inside Northern Ireland, the 'war zone'. To win that vital mass of support for its long-term political objective it was necessary to make big advances south of the Border. As the Green Book spelt out, they needed to create support *during* the time of armed action which would 'support us past the "Brits out" stage to the ultimate aim of a Democratic Socialist Republic.' In short, this meant dropping abstention and taking seats in Leinster House, where Dáil

Éireann sat. A move of that kind would represent a a shift of earthquake proportions, capabable of opening up yet another split in the Republican movement.

The abstention issue had been central to the IRA split and formation of the Provisional Army Council back in December 1969. It was the defining issue which permitted Thomas Maguire, the last surviving member of the 1921 Dáil Executive, to confer legitimacy on the Provisional Army Council. The matter was firmly enshrined in the Constitution of Óglaigh na hÉireann (IRA) and, as such, a two-thirds majority was needed to change it. The policy was set out in Section 1:

> Participation in Leinster House, Stormont or Westminster is strictly forbidden and in any other subservient Parliament, if any. Any volunteer who, by resolution proposes entry into Leinster House, Stormont or Westminster automatically dismisses himself from membership of Óglaigh na hÉireann.

Sinn Féin had a similar constitutional bar. At the time of its launch in 1970 the then caretaker executive of Sinn Féin said their task was 'to lead the Irish people away from British Six County and 26-County parliaments and towards the re-assembly of the 32-County Dáil ...'

Ruairí Ó Brádaigh, Dave O'Connell and their group would stay with this sacred policy to the grave. But they had been replaced by the brash pragmatists of the 'war zone'. Adams and McGuinness had no intention of remaining locked in and politically isolated like their predecessors. They knew it suited their political opponents south of the Border that they stay out of Dáil Éireann. Adams had seen an opportunity squandered in 1981, during the emotion of the hunger strikes. Two hunger strikers won seats in the Irish general election of that year which resulted in a split Dáil. The figures meant that had these two taken their seats they could have held the balance of power, determining that Charles Haughey and Fianna Fáil stay in office rather than be replaced by Dr FitzGerald's coalition government. Such leverage could have significantly affected Dublin's Northern Ireland policy.

The Adams leadership was determined to be free of such political rigidity. They pressed for the constitutional change and worked to nail down the vote for the necessary General Army Convention. They had one potent, secret weapon of persuasion, and strong persuasion would be required. There would be the inevitable charge that the dropping of abstention would lead the Republican movement into constitutional politics and away from the armed campaign: just as happened with Goulding's Officials, MacBride's Clann na Poblachta and de Valera's Fianna Fáil. The opposite would be the case, it was argued.

A small coterie of IRA leaders knew about the massive shipments of arms from Libya, then being finalised. They could promise waverers in the ranks that the IRA campaign would scale up not down, and that plans were in hand to deliver on that promise. As yet, in 1985, the Libyan arms deal was a tightly kept secret, but as some of the weapons arrived certain volunteers were given sight of spanking new modern hardware. It was persuasive.

The intended year for the change on abstention was 1985 but the leadership ran into dificulties and could not be sure of the required two-thirds majority. A move against the Adams leadership was crushed and the instigators, among them Ivor Bell, expelled from the IRA. Whatever else, a split in the IRA was to be avoided; it must come *en bloc*, with the dissenters still inside.

The next year, in October 1986, a General Army

Convention made the constitutional change. The vote was about 75 percent to 25 percent, This left a sizeable group of dissenters, some of them the hardest of militarists, who would watch future developments closely. There had been serious division in the South Armagh/Dundalk camp and outright opposition from Kerry and Mid-Ulster. The *quid pro quo* for opponents was that hardline militarists were brought on to the Army Council, with Martin McGuinness being given a pivotal role. Local units were to be given more freedom of action, 'local commander perogative' as it was called.

Sinn Féin followed suit, at their Árd Fheis in Dublin's Mansion House on 2 November 1986, after another intensive period of arm-twisting and debate. Delegates voted 429 to 161 to abandon their abstention policy regarding Dáil Éireann. The vote by the IRA Convention the previous month was decisive for many in the civil wing. It allowed the argument to be made, as McGuinness did, that those who walk away from the change also walk away from the armed struggle.

THE CONTINUITY ARMY COUNCIL

Some did walk away. Ruairí Ó Brádaigh and Dave O'Connell led a group out of the Mansion House and to a hotel in north Dublin where they announced the formation of Republican Sinn Féin. Ó Brádaigh was warned not to set up a rival army. Within a short time, however, a 'Continuity Army Council' (CAC) was established by a reconstituted Army Executive, offering allegiance to the principles held by Republican Sinn Féin. It was claimed that a majority on the existing IRA Executive had voted against Adams's move on abstention, that the Army Convention decision was therefore illegal and that the reconstituted Executive held the necessary 'continuity' of authority. It would be a number of years before the 'Continuity Army Council' showed its hand.

However, on 22 October 1986, immediately after the IRA Convention decision, 'Commdt General' Thomas Maguire intervened for the second time in sixteen years. In a public statement he withdrew his recognition from the Provisional Army Council. Nine months later, on 25 July 1987, Maguire went further and formally conferred 'legitimacy' on the new group:

> 'I hereby declare that the Continuity Executive and Continuity Army Council are the lawful Executive and Army Council respectively of the Irish Republican Army and that the governmental authority, delegated in the Proclamation of 1938, now resides in the Continuity Army Council and its lawful successors.'

For reasons of security, this latter statement was not made public until January 1996, when the Continuity Army Council first revealed itself.

Here was another classic republican split, though in 1986 it was generally regarded more as a shedding, with Ó Brádaigh's group presented as an insignificant remnant.

THE PROVISIONALS PLEDGE VICTORY

The depth and breadth of Gerry Adams's victory at the Sinn Féin Árd Fheis was illustrated by the catalogue of hard men and militarists including some from past and present campaigns who supported the change on abstention. Among them were Gerry Adams, Martin McGuinness, Pat Doherty, Joe Cahill, John Joe McGirl, JB O'Hagan and Seamus Twomey. The constant theme at the Árd Fheis had been that the armed campaign would continue until victory. When it was all over, the leadership of the Republican movement made this pledge in a Sinn Féin publication marking the 1986 decision:

> ... the decision was taken against the background of a unique and continuing armed struggle to which the IRA is not only committed, but which it pledges will be intensified until Britain declares that it is withdrawing from Ireland.

Did not the IRA now lack legitimacy and justification for armed force, having abandoned the sacred ground? The accusation was certainly made – and dismissed. Years and years of belief, the very bedrock of belief and justification now counted for nothing. There was history itself to fall back on. 'To suggest that the IRA is not legitimate because of the decision it has taken on abstention is ridiculous,' said an IRA statement of 5 November 1986. 'Our legitimacy stems from organised popular resistance to British rule in Ireland ... a tradition of resistance which has been a fact of history since Britain first encroached on Irish sovereignty 800 years ago.'

What of Sinn Féin's electoral prospects south of the Border, in the 'Free State' as they continued to deride it. What difference would the change make? During the debate on abstention, Gerry Adams predicted that Sinn Féin would win seats to Dáil Éireann and that the general election after the next one would be 'the first serious test of our ability to win major support.' In the follow-up statement of 5 November, the IRA leadership expressed confidence that 'Sinn Féin will emerge as a significant force in the Free State.' Privately Martin McGuinness predicted that Sinn Féin could win up to forty seats in Dáil Éireann. So, confidence was expressed all round that Sinn Féin would win big support in the south and in the north the IRA would force a British withdrawal.

THE STRATEGY FALTERS

Neither of those predictions came true. The period open-ing up would force yet another change of course by the IRA leadership. By then the 1990s were upon them, a new millenium was beckoning and still no victory was in sight. Back in 1987, however, the Libyan arms were in the process of being moved north. Commanders and quarter-masters were in place and a newly dedicated Army Council at the helm. The British military were geared up too, pre-pared to meet fire with fire. Learning from the lessons of the Stalker episode, when IRA activists had been shot dead while unarmed and apparently innocent, the practice now would be to shoot-to-kill only when the targets were 'on the job'.

In May 1987 came a spectacular example of this. Two combined IRA Active Service Units from around Monaghan and Mid-Tyrone were ambushed by the SAS in the tiny north Armagh village of Loughgall. The IRA men had arrived, carrying a bomb in the jaws of a mechanical digger, blew up Loughgall police station and were immediately shot down by massive fire. Eight IRA activists and a passing civilian were killed. It was the biggest single IRA loss since the 1920s. The dead included some of the IRA's most experienced opera-tives, the kind who were almost irreplaceable, like the unit's leader Jim Lynagh from Monaghan town, a lethal operator known to local Gardaí as 'The Executioner'.

This was the first in a series of setbacks. The seizure of the *Eksund* arms ship off France came in October 1987. Next month in Enniskillen, Co Fermanagh, on Remem-brance Sunday, 8 November, the IRA inflicted massive damage on its own twin-track strategy. Eleven people, ten civilians and a former RUC officer, died and sixty civilians were injured in a huge blast at the War memorial. Outrage was deep, emotional, sustained and widespread, especially among the Catholic population north and south. It was a huge undermining of the very constituency where Sinn Féin planned to make their electoral gains. Gerry Adams was forced to admit that the Republican movement could not withstand another Enniskillen episode. There was no deviation from the armed campaign, however. Later that month, on 23 November, the Irish police began their countrywide search for the Libyan arms, disrupting IRA movements, already disordered by the security follow-up to the Enniskillen massacre.

Over the next few months, into 1988, the number of arms finds increased as the IRA continued to move the Libyan weaponry into the 'war zone'. The discovery of 100 Kalashnikov rifles, 100lbs of Semtex explosives and a great deal more at Five Fingers Strand in remote north Donegal on 27 January 1988, was proof that the Libyan arms were in and being prepared for action. Other hauls came in Portmarnock, Co Dublin, Ballivor, Co Meath, Patrickswell, Co Limerick, more in Donegal. Hides and bunkers were uncovered and Kalashnikovs found on the outskirts of Belfast. Internal inquiries into these seizures stalled IRA operations and aroused suspicions. One man, the quartermaster for the Belfast Brigade with overall responsibility for the city's arms and explosives, was found to have been an informer for up to eight years.

Then, on 6 March 1988, the SAS shot dead three IRA activists in Gibraltar, ostensibly in the act of blowing up a British Army band parade there. Gibraltar was to have been an IRA 'spectacular', the kind that shows they can strike anywhere at any time. This would have had special significance. It would constitute a sort of 'thank you' to Col Ghadaffi for the arms and a strike of the right anti-imperialist kind at a British outpost in the Mediterranean. The fact that the three dead – Seán Savage, Danny McCann and Mairead Farrell – were unarmed brought a propaganda harvest to the Republican movement somewhat offsetting the Enniskillen debacle. But the IRA leadership knew that Gibraltar was a serious operational failure, not least because it was clear that British intelligence had known about it for months. Gibraltar was to have been the IRA's launching pad for the much-awaited escalation. Instead of a glorious triumph, a great boost to morale and expectations, there were three more martyrs to place on the roll of honour.

FAILING ON THE POLITICAL FRONT

It was also clear that the Republican movement's political momentum had stalled too. By 1989, north and south, Sinn Féin was stuck. Major gains had been made in Belfast. In some areas their fortunes went into reverse. Sinn Féin had become a permanent political fixture. Yet their challenge to the SDLP in Northern Ireland was beaten back and the gap widened in favour of John Hume's brand of democratic politics. The pattern was the same in District Council, Westminster and European elections. Sinn Féin was stuck at around 11 percent of the vote with the SDLP at around 21 percent. The biggest defeat came in the 1989 European election when John Hume reached a new high of 25 percent. His Sinn Féin rival, Danny Morrison, got a mere 9 percent of the vote, a new low.

In the Republic Sinn Féin's performance was dismal in the extreme. During the 1986 debate on abstention, Adams had promised big gains within two general elections. In the first of those tests, the 1987 election, Sinn Féin came out with 1.7 percent of the first preference vote and no seats. But in the next general election in 1989, Sinn Féin's vote was even more insignificant, at 1.2 percent and no seats. The cause – the IRA's deeply unpopular armed campaign – was clear.

Another political door was closed in 1989. Hopes that Fianna Fáil might dump the the Anglo–Irish Agreement were dashed. The Agreement was due for review that year. Back in government, Taoiseach Charles Haughey reaffirmed its contents in tandem with the British government. The Republican movement was facing a wall.

There was no forseeable prospect of the 1986 promises being realised, militarily or politically. They could do no more on their own and could only make progress on their agenda by building political alliances and even re-examining the armed struggle. It was a process which had already begun. Formal talks between the SDLP and Sinn Féin took place from March to September 1988. They ended in failure, the SDLP refusing to contemplate a common strategy while the IRA campaign continued. Hume and Adams, however, agreed to continue their dialogue. That dialogue would become highly significant as time went on. Other movements were in the air too. Peter Brooke became Secretary of State for Northern Ireland in July 1989. He would soon make a huge contribution to attitudes within the IRA. So too would the loyalist paramilitaries. They had been re-arming with modern weapons from South African sources, partly assisted, it seemed, by elements in British intelligence. The next chapter would be bloody and historic.

INTO THE PEACE PROCESS, 1990–1994

The Provisional IRA had been in existence for twenty years as the 1990s opened. Just as the men of 1916 would have scarcely believed it possible that Ireland would still be partitioned, the original Provisional Army Council never imagined an armed campaign of this duration. By the start of 1990 the Provisionals had killed 1,593 people and wounded more than 15,000. Their bombings had continued unabated, terrorising and destroying: 258 bombs in 1987; 304 bombs in 1988; 269 bombs in 1989. Their justification for the use of force was no longer rooted in the claim of holding the 'powers of government' of the Republic. That claim had been tarnished and undermined by the events of 1986, though volunteers were still being 'Green Booked' as though nothing had changed. Sacred principles had been cast aside on the altar of pragmatism. The IRA had returned to bedrock for its legitimacy, that of resisting British rule in Ireland. They could trumpet a certain mandate, votes won for Sinn Féin in the north, especially in Belfast. But by that same yardstick about 95 percent of the people on the island did not support them, rejecting them in most part.

Crucially, the British government's policy of 'normalisation' and 'criminalisation' was successful and effectively permanent. They had long-since blocked the IRA's ambition to force the introduction of military rule in Northern Ireland. Britain had regularly updated its Emergency Provisions Act, retaining non-jury courts, ending the 'right of silence' for suspects, introducing genetic fingerprinting, curtailing access to the broadcasting airwaves, granting to police and courts the power to confiscate paramilitary finances. All emergency legislation applying to Northern Ireland was brought together in one Act in 1991. The rule of British law was entrenched.

The IRA could sustain its campaign into the indefinite future. That much was agreed. Yet, in all the circumstances, the Republican movement was examining its options and concluding that the armed struggle would not deliver victory. They would have to settle for 'interim arrangements' and leave the rest to politics. British withdrawal was not achieved but a process of irreversible change was expected. The IRA would not surrender, however, nor be *seen* to surrender.

All of this was slow and tortuous in coming. In its first phase it took from 1990 to 1994 to complete. It required involvement in an intricate web of political contacts and bridge-building in Ireland, Britain and the United States. Crucially it meant forging new alliances with John Hume and the 'illegal puppet' government in Dublin. History was truly made in those years as the IRA moved to a complete cessation. Even though the bombs came out again in 1996 and much pessimism returned, the IRA remained engaged in the Irish peace process.

NO STRATEGIC INTEREST

Two political events within a fortnight of each other in November 1990 led to a sea-change in the Irish conflict. Both occurred in Britain. The first, on 9 November, was a speech by the Northern Secretary, Peter Brooke, in his London constituency of Westminster. Brooke made a direct pitch for the hearts and minds of the Republican movement, putting down an historic marker about Britain's role in Northern Ireland. The second event, on 22 November, was cataclysmic. Margaret Thatcher resigned as Conservative Party leader and British Prime Minister, having failed to win the required majority in a leadership challenge. She was replaced five days later by John Major, a pragmatic politician who would come to put his weight behind a significant Irish peace initiative.

In his speech Peter Brooke addressed the questions of the 'Unionist veto' and the 'British presence', both targets of the IRA campaign and obstacles to Irish unity. Brooke acknowledged that the aspiration to a United Ireland had integrity and could be legitimately pursued by peaceful means, though not 'by the cruel and brutal methods of violence and coercion'. At the end of a lengthy analysis the Northern Secretary came up with a highly charged statement, resounding with great potential significance for the IRA (and Irish nationalists generally). 'The British government', he said, 'has no selfish, strategic or economic interest in Northern Ireland: our role is to help, enable and encourage.'

The prospect of significant change was implied, provided the use of force was out of the equation. This, in turn, prompted a considered reply from Gerry Adams. Serious dialogue was in the air. Adams defended the tactic of armed struggle but also challenged other nationalists to come up with a viable alternative in the context of Britain being neutral on the Union. Debate within the Republican movement was intensified. Hopes were raised even to the point that Peter Brooke might have begun the first move towards a British withdrawal. They were disappointed. At the 1992 Sinn Féin Árd Fheis, Northern Organiser, Jim Gibney, put it this way: 'We opened our minds to his words. We dared to hope that he would be the first British Secretary of State who would begin the healing process between all the Irish people and ultimately between Ireland and Britain by starting the disengagement process.'

This was a profoundly naive view of the prevailing political realities. The expectation that Britain would begin a 'disengagement process' because of armed force was what fuelled the IRA's campaign. Their analysis dictated that unionism or loyalism had no legitimacy but was merely an opportunistic junior partner to the British government. Armed force was necessary to prise them apart. 'Brits out', the first stage, having been accomplished, Unionists would discover their true Irish heritage and take their rightful place in a United Ireland.

All of this reflected the traditional Irish nationalist view down the years. But by the 1990s the Republican movement was virtually on its own in that regard. A new bedrock position had been reached to which the Irish government and most northern nationalists subscribed, namely that there would be no change in the constitutional status of Northern Ireland without the consent of a majority of its people. That bedrock principle was enshrined in the Sunningdale Agreement of 1973 and the Anglo–Irish Agreement of 1985. The IRA had opposed both of these by force on the grounds that there could be no 'Unionist veto' on the full exercise of Irish national self-determination. That view hadn't changed. It was *their* bedrock position. What was being sought by Peter Brooke was that the Republican movement pursue its objectives without armed force.

For his part, Brooke was declaring Britain to be neutral on the Union, to have no interests of her own in being in Northern Ireland, and that the IRA's real opponents were the Unionists not the British government. The IRA would have to focus on the rights and aspirations of the Unionist people. It would require a virtual abandonment of the long war's basic analysis. But that was the road which was opening up.

BOMBS AND COMPROMISE

Within the Republican movement an intensive debate was under way. An outward sign of this had been the three-day ceasefire over Christmas 1990, the first for many years and a sign of interest in what Peter Brooke had to say. During 1991 strategies were being examined. Shifts were taking place, not in the basic objective but in the means of getting there. A broadly held view was developing within the leadership that Britain was no longer in Northern Ireland pursuing her own strategic interests. This raised questions about the value of armed struggle or, more importantly, whether armed struggle should end before a British declaration to withdraw had been won. The Army Council was divided over when to stop, at one point voting by four to three in favour of continuing the armed campaign. Permitting this debate was in itself a major shift and also a risk, that it would be regarded as a sign of weakness. The fact was that by the end of 1991 the IRA leadership had set off on a course to ceasefire and compromise.

As always, the IRA would exert as much pressure as possible. Their tactical aim was two-fold: to end the 'Unionist veto' and to secure an unconditional place for Sinn Féin at the negotiating table. The IRA leadership had looked to South Africa as the principal model for this development. There, Nelson Mandela's ANC refused to give up armed struggle prior to entering talks with T W De Klerk's white government and forswore violence only when negotiations had produced sufficient momentum to guarantee change.

Things would not be so neat and tidy for the IRA, however. They were in many respects captives of their own long war strategy. The Adams–McGuinness leadership had promised a British withdrawal. Now, a decade and a half later, they were faced with ending the armed campaign while British rule remained intact. The process of change would be slow, personally risky and capable of producing the much-dreaded split. For the moment, force would still be used as a direct political lever, aimed at moving Britain a good deal further on the issue of Irish self-determination.

On 7 February 1991 an IRA mortar bomb exploded right inside the Downing Street security curtain, within yards of where John Major and his Cabinet were meeting. No-one was injured but the attack was a major propaganda and logistical triumph, carrying an IRA message right to the heart of the British establishment. It would mark the new phase of direct pressure on Britain, trying to prise further the door already opened by Peter Brooke.

So while the IRA leadership was preparing to enter political dialogue they were also gearing up for a bombing offensive in Britain and in Northern Ireland. This time, the essential difference with the past was that the IRA was thrusting to get *in* to talks rather than trying to destroy them. This position reflected a growing mood within their own communities, to end the conflict on the streets. These republican areas were under renewed pressure from the loyalist camp. Re-equipped and re-organised loyalist para-military groups, the UDA and UVF, had upped the tempo of their killing campaign. In 1991 they killed 40, compared to 47 by the IRA and in 1992, for the first time, loyalist killings outstripped those of the IRA. The loyalists made it plain that they would strike in retaliation for IRA killings, placing added pressure on local IRA leaders and activists.

HUME–ADAMS

In between, significant political dialogue was taking place both publicly and in high secrecy. The British and Irish governments were getting a three-stranded negotiating process under way, involving both governments and the northern constitutional parties. These negotiations began at Stormont buildings, Belfast, in June 1991. The talks sought an agreement covering new political structures within Northern Ireland, between north and south and between Britain and Ireland: three interlocking strands. Such a formula pre-supposed the continued existence of Northern Ireland and a continued British presence there. Significantly Sinn Féin began to demand a place at these negotiations on the basis of their electoral mandate. This demand was the clearest sign of the Republican movement's shift of emphasis and a reflection of other, totally confidential, moves taking place.

Secretly, John Hume was engaged in a process with Gerry Adams who was acting with authority for the Army Council. These face-to-face talks had the potential to end the IRA campaign, get Sinn Féin to the negotiating table and heal the schism in Irish nationalism north and south. It was historic stuff, not least because the process involved the then head of the Irish government, Charles Haughey. Hume sought Haughey's support for the main aim of his talks with Adams, namely a 'Joint Declaration', the first draft of which appeared in October 1991. The concept was that the British and Irish governments would sign up to this 'Joint Declaration', giving expression to the right and exercise of Irish self-determination in a form of words strong enough to convince the IRA to call a halt. There was no guarantee of success and a real risk that, if discovered, the entire project would blow up in the faces of Hume and Haughey, particularly as the IRA's bombing and killing campaign had been stepped up.

Both directly and through an agreed senior British official, John Chilcott, Hume kept the British Prime Minister informed of his dealings with Adams. John Major did not discourage the process. In all of this the IRA was holding out for a commitment from Britain to acknowledge the Irish people's right to national self-determination. At issue between Hume and Adams was how to square this 'right' with the divided allegiances of the people on the island of Ireland, how to accommodate the Unionists' British allegiance. However it was done, the IRA was intent on diminishing the separate 'right' of Northern Ireland in any agreed Joint Declaration. In effect this meant coercing the Unionists.

Pursuing their objective, the IRA began 1992 with massive bombs and horrendous killings. Belfast city centre suffered huge destruction from an 800lb IRA bomb on 3 January and from a 500lb bomb two days later. Then on 17 January a roadside bomb at Teebane Cross in the Tyrone countryside blew up a minibus, killing eight of the fourteen Protestant workmen travelling home. In IRA parlance the men were 'executed' as 'collaborators', having worked on a British Army base, part of long-running IRA tactics. Public outrage was immense, anger was black, almost on a par with that following the Enniskillen bomb back in 1987. Teebane brought direct loyalist retaliation in deadly fashion. On 5 February the Ulster Freedom Fighters (UFF) did a 'spray' job at a bookmakers on Belfast's Ormeau Road, killing five ordinary Catholics and citing the Teebane Cross massacre as the reason.

The IRA atrocities were not aimed at getting a British withdrawal but at advancing the complicated political process secretly under way. The next month, February 1992, the Republican movement provided public evidence, for internal as well as external consumption, that change was in the air. At the Sinn Féin Árd Fheis in Dublin, Adams launched a new political blueprint, a detailed document titled *Towards a Lasting Peace*. In a nutshell, the document paved the way for an alliance with the Irish government and the SDLP, provided they moved in the direction of seeking national self-determination. Importantly, the document focused on the needs of the Unionists and obliquely opened up the prospect of ending the armed campaign in pursuit of an interim settlement. The key would be a move by Britain to a policy position of seeking Irish unity.

The British were showing their mettle too. Their toughened policy of shooting dead IRA activists caught on the job had continued apace. At the February 1992 Árd Fheis seven new names appeared on the 'roll of honour', three armed activists mown down by undercover British forces at Coagh village, Co Tyrone, the previous June; and, just days before the Sinn Féin meeting, four more were shot dead by massive gunfire in an ambush at Clonoe Catholic Church grounds, also in Co Tyrone. The four activists, with others, had returned from a brazen mission, where they riddled Coalisland police station, using a huge 12.7mm Russian DHSK machine gun, part of the Libyan shipment.

The IRA had its own massive pressure, awaiting application. On 10 April 1992, a month after the launch of Sinn Féin's 'peace' document, colossal destruction was caused in London's financial centre. An IRA bomb at the Baltic Exchange killed three people but left in its wake a huge area of smashed high-rise buildings. The compensation damage for this one bomb, estimated at more than £600million, was more than the entire compensation payout in Northern Ireland to that point.

Meanwhile, the move to an agreed 'Joint Declaration' had gathered considerable momentum. A new Taoiseach in Dublin, Albert Reynolds, who had replaced Haughey in January 1992, took up the secret initiative with a rare confidence that the IRA *could* be brought in from the cold against all the odds. It was a high risk strategy, given that the IRA was illegal and viewed with extreme distaste and hostility by almost the entire Irish population. Reynolds carried on the dialogue through John Hume and Haughey's former adviser, Martin Mansergh. The conduit through which they all worked was Fr Alex Reid of Clonard Monastery, Belfast. Reid also sat in on all the meetings between Hume and Adams. By June 1992 the IRA Army Council had put its weight behind the proposed Declaration. They would settle for a form of words and a political process and, *ipso facto*, end their long war without a British withdrawal. It was a breathtaking prospect and one which, at the time, was known to only a handful of people inside and outside the Republican movement.

THE IRA'S PEACE PROPOSAL

In June 1992 the final wording of a draft 'Joint Declaration' was approved by the IRA Army Council and submitted to the Irish government, via Sinn Féin. The proposal was, in effect, a combined Hume–Adams–Reynolds document, the fruit of several drafts and many meetings. It became in time an Irish government proposal to the British government, though there was a year and much anguish, death and destruction to come before it was submitted. The document was headed:

> Draft of a declaration which Sinn Féin suggests should be made jointly by the British and Dublin governments.

It had eight sections and covered two typed pages. The extent and depth of the new thinking could be seen in Section 2, dealing with Europe. It said the Taoiseach and Prime Minister:

> ... consider that the development of European Union fundamentally changes the nature and the context of British–Irish relationships and will progressively remove the basis of the historic conflict still taking place in Northern Ireland.

That analysis, in itself, raised basic questions for the IRA Army Council. If changes in Europe 'will progressively remove the basis of the historic conflict' what further justification could there be for armed struggle? The IRA, however, would continue to use force as a political lever.

Throughout, the language was a far cry from the simple certainties of 'Brits out' strategy contained in the Green Book. The whole context was the settling of relationships within Ireland, north and south, and between the two islands: fitting exactly the three-stranded political process then in progress. Section 3 had both prime ministers recognising:

> ... that the ending of divisions can come about only through the agreement and cooperation of the people, North and South, representing both traditions in Ireland ... It is their aim to foster agreement and reconciliation, leading to a new political framework founded on consent and encompassing the whole island.

In a major break with the past and with the entire long war strategy, the document did not contain a British declaration of intent to withdraw from Northern Ireland. However, in a complex set of words the proposed 'Joint Declaration' had the British government making a significant political move towards a policy of accepting and encouraging Irish self-determination. But crucially, as a balance, the Irish government would acknowledge the separate right of consent for the people of Northern Ireland. In other words, the IRA was prepared to accept the separate need for consent within Northern Ireland provided this was an *Irish* and not a British concession. That was the key. It opened up the prospect of a major compromise and a purely political phase in the 'struggle', during which the objectives would be the pursuit of consent and a process of national reconciliation. Taken together, Sections 4 and 5 amounted to a huge shift by the IRA leadership. They read, in full:

4. The British Prime Minister reiterates on behalf of the British government, that they have no selfish, strategic, political or economic interest in Northern Ireland, and that their sole interest is to see peace, stability and reconciliation established by agreement among the people who inhabit the island. The British government accepts the principle that the Irish people have the right collectively to self-determination and that the exercise of this right could take the form of agreed independent structures for the island as a whole. They affirm their readiness to introduce the measures to give legislative effect on their side to this right (within a specified period to be agreed) and allowing sufficient time for the building of consent and the beginning of a process of national reconciliation. The British government will use all its influence and energy to win the consent of a majority in Northern Ireland for these measures. They acknowledge that it is the wish of the people of Britain to see the people of Ireland live together in unity and harmony, but with full recognition of the special links and the unique relationship which exists between the peoples of Britain and Ireland.

5. The Taoiseach, on behalf of the Irish government, considers that the lessons of Irish history and especially of Northern Ireland, show that stability and well-being will not be found under any political system which is refused allegiance or rejected on grounds of identity by a significant minority of those governed by it. He accepts, on behalf of the Irish government, that the democratic right of self-determination by the people of Ireland as a whole

> must be achieved and exercised with the agreement and consent
> of the people of Northern Ireland and must, consistent with jus-
> tice and equity, respect the democratic dignity and the civil rights
> of both communities.

In its final element, the document referred to a proposed 'permanent Irish Convention', set up under the Irish Con-stitution, with the task of consulting and advising on the steps needed to build trust between Ireland's divided people. This Section 7 stated that it would be a 'fundame-ntal guiding principle' of the Convention that differences in Ireland regarding self-determination 'will be resolved exclusively by peaceful, political means.'

Without doubt the IRA Army Council was committing itself to an indefinite ceasefire on the back of this proposal. As yet it was an Irish nationalist agenda. The question was, would Britain buy in?

CONTINUING THE AGONY

With the big move made, the IRA set about increasing the pressure on the British government. Their campaign of attrition, of course, continued as before with daily small-scale attacks, bombs of various kinds, hijackings and kid-nappings, more failures than successes. But far bigger bangs were necessary to catch attention. Following a short-age of nitrobenzine, a vital bomb-making ingredient, the IRA discovered a new mix based on a very common chemical. This allowed them to move to a new high impact bombing phase as time would show.

All the while, political and military action was becoming increasingly intertwined. Secret contacts between a British government representative, code-named 'the Mountain Climber', and the IRA/Sinn Féin, principally Martin McGuinness, had been re-opened. During 1992 briefings by the British to McGuinness were intensified. They were to lead in early 1993 to a British proposal for formal two-week talks in a foreign location, combined with a fourteen-day IRA ceasefire, at the end of which the IRA would be convinced that 'armed struggle was no longer necessary'. There was tempting talk from the British side that the future was one of 'union' between both parts of Ireland. As it happened, mysterious premature disclosure of these secret contacts in late 1993 ended that particular process in a welter of accusation and counter-accusation between Sinn Féin and the British government. But the contacts convinced the IRA leadership of two vital things: first, that Britain would talk to Sinn Féin without a perma-nent IRA cessation; and secondly, though less supported by the facts, that Britain wanted to disengage from North-ern Ireland. These beliefs were enough to sustain IRA morale, conviction and determination at a high level.

In between all of this, a British general election returned John Major as Prime Minister (April 1992), a 2,000lb IRA bomb destroyed the Northern Ireland foren-sic science laboratories in Belfast (September 1992), another destroyed the centre of Bangor (October 1992), Bill Clinton became US President promising an Irish peace initiative (November 1992), the three-stranded political talks ended in failure (November 1992), Albert Reynolds returned as Taoiseach of a new Fianna Fáil-Labour Coalition with an historically large majority (January 1993), a 500lb IRA bomb hit Bangor again (March 1993), an IRA bomb in Warrington, England, killed two children, leading to worldwide condemnation (March 1993), a massive IRA bomb caused huge destruc-tion at Bishopsgate, London's financial centre (April 1993).

Despite all their 'pressure' the pace of political progress was slow and Britain's attitude uncertain. In a written communication passed to the Irish government, dated 13 April 1993, the IRA Army Council expressed 'concern at the protracted nature of this process'. At the same time they reaffirmed their commitment to the proposed 'Joint Declaration'. 'We are very serious about this project,' they wrote. 'We recognise that what is required is a package which creates a political dynamic for irreversible change and whose objective is the exercise of the right to national self-determination.' The 'dynamic' was an agreed timescale for the process, a central demand which would not be achieved but which would prolong the IRA's bombing offensive. This was an attempt by the IRA to get a cut-off point for arriving at consent in Northern Ireland, a device for ending the 'Unionist veto' through negotiations.

The IRA's hopes for a short timescale, say two to five years, was a long way from Dublin's expectations. In their April communication, the Army Council complained to Dublin about the Irish government's 'understanding' that the timescale for the exercise of self-determination could be anywhere between fifteen and forty years. These differences were kept hidden for tactical reasons, the IRA wanting to keep the public focus on Britain. For the moment, a strong nationalist consensus had emerged in the form of the proposed 'Joint Declaration' and in June 1993 the Irish government submitted it to London, with small changes of emphasis.

At first the Republican movement leadership agonised over the significance of the compromise to which they had put their name. They even withdrew their support for a short period, fearing the consequences of a British acceptance, before getting back on board again. That same month, on 20 June, Martin McGuinness gave the first public indication of the huge change of direction being contemplated. Speaking to the faithful at the annual Wolfe Tone commemoration at Bodenstown, McGuinness spoke about the 'deep fears' of the Unionists:

> 'We need to address those fears honestly and we accept that interim arrangements to allay understandable concerns may be required to facilitate the establishment of a dynamic Irish democracy.'

'Interim arrangements' was a momentous phrase, signalling as it clearly did that the IRA would stop a very long way short of a British withdrawal. Here was a signal admission that twenty-two years of force had failed to dislodge the British.

Neither had they built a supportive mass movement south of the Border, as planned and promised: 'No one can deny that, with honourable exceptions, we have generally failed to make any significant impact on the political map of the twenty-six counties,' acknowledged McGuinness in his Bodenstown oration. To move forward within a reasonable timespan the Republican movement needed the support and leadership of the Irish government, though at a price.

From that point Sinn Féin went on a 'peace' offensive. They agitated around the 'Irish Peace Initiative', as they styled the as yet unpublished Hume–Adams–Reynolds proposal. As usual, the IRA continued parallel military activity. They exploded huge destructive bombs in the centres of Belfast, Magherafelt, Portadown and Newtownards during May to July 1993. There was also a direct threat of more bombs in London. In a crude attempt to increase pressure on John Major the IRA made public a letter they had sent to foreign-owned financial institutions there. It laid out the basic move being sought from the British government for an IRA cessation, acceptance of the Irish people's 'immutable right' to national self-determination. 'The acceptance of that right by Britain would initiate a peace process which can finally end this long-running war,' the letter said.

A combined force of Irish nationalists was asking a great deal of the British Prime Minister at precisely the time his government was under increased reliance on the votes of Unionist MPs at Westminster. In any event, British intelligence analysis had it that the IRA would not call a cessation and, further, that their campaign would wither over time. So John Major stalled and delayed while Albert Reynolds and John Hume piled on the pressure. With the IRA signed up to the secret 'Joint Declaration' proposal Reynolds and Hume were convinced that a total end to the armed campaign was in the offing.

The IRA themselves almost derailed the entire project with a bomb in the heart of the Protestant Shankill Road, Belfast, on 23 October 1993. The explosion killed ten civilians and injured fifty-eight. The target had been a loyalist paramilitary meeting place but the bomb, exploding prematurely, wrecked a busy fish shop. In the midst of massive tension and condemnation, the loyalist UFF/UDA retaliated in kind seven days later. At a Catholic bar in Greysteel, Co Derry, eight people were shot dead in another indiscriminate 'spray job'.

The 'Joint Declaration' proposal could well have died at that point. But after huge pressure from Dublin and the near-collapse of the initiative through extreme British reluctance, Reynolds and Major finally agreed a 'Joint Declaration'. It was unveiled at 10 Downing Street on 15 December 1993. By any reckoning it represented an historic statement by the British government. It also demanded further compromise from the IRA. Their hand was being forced.

THE IRA RESPONDS

For many IRA activists the 'Joint Declaration' made confusing and pessimistic reading. It was not what they had fought for, been imprisoned for, seen others die for. The 'Joint Declaration' was not a 'Brits out' prescription. Worse, it seemed to copper-fasten the 'Unionist veto' and envelop the principle of self-determination in a fog of confusion. Most early sentiment was rejectionist, probably about 90 for to 10 against, among the northern activists.

In Article 2 of the Declaration, both governments re-committed themselves to Northern Ireland's constitutional guarantee. The aim, as expressed, was to build a new political framework 'encompassing arrangements within Northern Ireland, for the whole island and between these islands'. Article 4 dealing with self-determination was the key. It represented a substantial shift by the British government, in effect to a one-island approach to the Irish problem. But firmly embedded in it was the separate right of the people of Northern Ireland to constitutional change. In that way the expressed 'right' of self-determination was qualified:

> The British government agree that it is for the people of the island of Ireland alone, by agreement between the two parts respectively, to exercise their right of self-determination on the basis of consent, freely and concurrently given, North and South, to bring about a united Ireland, if that is their wish.

This was a prescription for the British government to stand back, leaving constitutional decisions in the hands of the people of Northern Ireland and for any political settlement to be determined by concurrent referenda north and south. It would mean continued British jurisdiction over Northern Ireland and full recognition of that jurisdiction by the Republic of Ireland for the first time.

In line with the 'Irish Peace Initiative', Article 5 had the Taoiseach on behalf of the Irish government accepting that:

> ... the democratic right of self-determination by the people of Ire-
> land as a whole must be achieved and exercised with and subject to
> the agreement and consent of the people of Northern Ireland ...

The combined formula in the 'Joint Declaration' ensured that any agreed settlement would be both partitionist and all-Ireland 'with full recognition of the special links' (Article 4) between the peoples of Britain and Ireland. If they moved along that road, the IRA was facing into a significant and, for some, unacceptable compromise.

The IRA Army Council made one early crucial move. They decided not to reject the Declaration. This left vital room for manoeuvre. At the same time they continued exerting pressure with a view to extracting more: carrying out 15 shootings, four hijackings, 22 explosions, causing extensive damage by incendiary devices and killing one British soldier, all in the first six weeks after the Declaration.

In particular, the Army Council wanted a further shift by Britain, towards being 'persuaders' for Irish unity and also that any negotiations would contain the necessary 'dynamic' (ie, timescale) to ensure that a Unionist veto could not block progress. Just as importantly, the Republican movement leadership needed time for persuasion and debate within their own sceptical ranks. Given that the Hume–Adams–Reynolds dialogue had been top secret, the concepts contained in the 'Joint Declaration' were convoluted and disturbing to the rank and file.

DUBLIN AND WASHINGTON WAIT AND ACT

In Dublin, Albert Reynolds expected an IRA cessation by the end of February 1994 at the latest. Instead, after many twists and turns, mini-crises and fading patience, the IRA took until August to make the big move. Along the way, Dublin and Washington combined to build momentum behind the 'peace' group within the IRA and Sinn Féin. Reynolds worked to remove obstacles and to demonstrate that political action *could* deliver results. In January 1994 his government astounded the general public and London by lifting the Ministerial Directive under Section 31 of the Irish Broadcasting Act which for twenty-three years had banned Sinn Féin (and other paramilitary) spokespersons from the national airwaves. Reynolds also gave the IRA and Sinn Féin all the 'clarification' they sought during their heady propaganda drive. Some of this clarification firmly closed off IRA hopes that they could extract more on the issue of self-determination. In January 1994, Reynolds addressed this point, saying:

> 'It is not possible to insist that self-determination must have a guaranteed or pre-determined outcome. No example can be found anywhere in a long-divided country of the application of self-determination, except in the way set out in the Joint Declaration.'

But Reynolds was also promising something very tempting to the Republican movement. In his private and public contacts the Irish Prime Minister gave assurances, gave his 'word', that his government would seek to negotiate 'transitional' arrangements on the island of Ireland. This meant the construction of a transitional phase towards eventual

Irish independence, always provided that consent in Northern Ireland was forthcoming. It fitted in large measure with the IRA's concept of 'interim arrangements' and, as such, was extremely persuasive.

The American connection was persuasive too. There, a new Irish–American lobby had developed behind the Clinton candidature and his Presidency. This was no old-style 'Brits out' grouping but rather a sophisticated collection of politicians like Bruce Morrison and wealthy businessmen like Bill Flynn and Chuck Feeney. These were no closet Provos but men firmly committed to a significant US intervention, pressing the Republican movement for non-violence and Britain for equal rights. This lobby was resolutely behind the Reynolds approach of seeking constitutional 'balance' between the two conflicting allegiances in Ireland.

In early February 1994, President Clinton publicly rowed in too, taking 'risks for peace' as the phrase of the day had it. Clinton accepted the advice of Albert Reynolds and that of his White House National Security officials concerning a US visa application by Gerry Adams. Risking the wrath of the British government and his own State Department, both of whom vigorously opposed the application, Clinton granted a forty-eight hour visa to Gerry Adams to speak at a conference on Northern Ireland, hosted by the National Committee on Foreign Policy whose chairman was Bill Flynn. Adams had been excluded from the US since before he became Sinn Féin President in 1983, due to his espousal of political violence. He arrived to huge media exposure, further enhancing his standing back home; all the more so since the British government's nose had been put out of joint.

MOVING TO A CESSATION

There was still no certainty of an IRA cessation but momentum was gathering. The Sinn Féin Árd Fheis, also in February, passed a number of motions which the leadership interpreted as support for the still unpublished 'Irish Peace Initiative'. Meanwhile the IRA kept up its attempts to prise more from the process under way. On 9, 10 and 13 March 1994 the IRA launched a number of mortars on London's Heathrow Airport. None exploded but fear and panic was widespread. Albert Reynolds condemned the attack as 'politically naive'. In Washington on St Patrick's Day, 17 March, President Clinton called on the IRA to lay down their arms. IRA bombings continued within Northern Ireland but a sign of change came at Easter 1994 when the IRA called a three-day ceasefire. To the IRA this was a significant gesture, a sign of their interest in peace. In Dublin the ceasefire was met by bitter disappointment, a move worthy of no response.

The IRA leadership was becoming hemmed in. They had permitted a lengthy and open debate on the merits of continuing with armed struggle. Sentiment in the prisons, influenced by the likes of Danny Morrison and Bobby Storey, was shifting towards a ceasefire. This was the expectation within the heartlands too. But the 'Joint Declaration' was widely regarded as insufficient and, in any event, people focused on a temporary cessation of three or six months, not a permanent one. Activists and supporters were told there were no guarantees available, no certain united Ireland or British withdrawal. Still, the IRA leadership was holding out for a process containing an 'irreversible thrust' towards change across the island. However the leadership moved, it was a cardinal guiding principle that they would avoid a split.

These were tense and violent days. Loyalist paramilitary groups, now operating under a Combined Loyalist Military Command, were also considering a ceasefire while keeping the killing pressure going. They shot dead nine Catholics in Belfast, Tyrone and Armagh during April and May. At the end of May the UVF attempted mass slaughter at Dublin's Widow Scallan's pub during an IRA/Sinn Féin meeting but killed only one man, Martin Doherty, who stopped the bomb being primed. Then, on 16 June the quasi-Marxist republican group, the Irish National Liberation Army, struck in the heart of the loyalist Shankill Road in Belfast, killing two alleged UVF leaders, Colin Craig and David Hamilton. Three days later the UVF retaliated with a 'spray job' more akin to the tactics used by the Ulster Freedom Fighters. Six people were killed and five injured in a Catholic pub in Loughinisland, Co Down, as patrons watched the Republic of Ireland play Italy in the World Cup. On 11 July, the IRA made their own strike at loyalism, shooting dead Ray Smallwoods, one of the new breed of political thinkers within the UDA. It was as though old scores were being settled on all sides. Pessimism abounded. Obvious strains appeared within the Irish coalition government where the Labour leader Dick Spring was becoming increasingly impatient with IRA manoeuverings.

Albert Reynolds was becoming impatient too. In mid-July he sent a written communication to the IRA leadership, telling them they would have to decide, saying he had given two years of his life to the peace initiative, effectively laying down a deadline of early September for an IRA cessation but promising to bring Gerry Adams into Government Buildings within a week of such a cessation. By that stage the Republican movement leadership was almost evenly divided, some believing that more could be extracted from Britain by armed force. But there was a price to be paid for the new alliance with Dublin and they were now being asked to pay up.

Martin McGuinness, always a pivotal figure, was brought around, in part, by the influence of Reynolds's special advisor, Martin Mansergh (known as 'The Man' by his IRA/Sinn Féin contacts). The historic decision was made in late July and conveyed with great secrecy to Albert Reynolds. Among the leading political and military figures who brought the IRA to this historic juncture were Gerry Adams, Martin McGuinness, Pat Doherty, Joe Cahill, Kevin McKenna, Tom Murphy, Gerry Kelly and an outer ring which included Mitchel McLaughlin, Ted Howell, Danny Morrison and Bobby Storey. The IRA leadership had become convinced by the Adams–McGuinness political analysis that an historically strong nationalist consensus existed, backed by a powerful Irish–American lobby, which would ensure political and constitutional change in Ireland and which would, therefore, considerably advance the 'struggle' at that time without the need for armed force.

There was one more hurdle to be overcome within the Republican movement. Sinn Féin would be asked to endorse the historic decision taken by the 'supreme authority' of the movement, the IRA Army Council. This was done. At a special Sinn Féin Conference in Letterkenny, Co Donegal, on 24 July 1994 delegates passed a number of motions which, while not explicitly stated, amounted to an endorsement of the political analysis accepted by the IRA Army Council. Through a series of votes, Sinn Féin resolved to 'build upon' the 'Joint Declaration' and to work to bridge the 'gaps' between it and the 'Irish Peace Initiative.'

A COMPLETE CESSATION OF MILITARY OPERATIONS

The long war petered out over the next few weeks. Never without surprises, the IRA engaged in one last spectacular. On 18 August 1994 they assassinated leading Dublin criminal, Martin Cahill (known as 'The General'), claiming he had assisted the UVF in their bomb attempt on the Widow Scallan's pub. The last recorded incident was a mortar attack on Fort Whiterock British army base in Belfast at 11pm on Tuesday, 30 August 1994. By that stage the history-making cessation statement had been put together and cleared in conjunction with Albert Reynolds's office. Reynolds wanted to be sure that the phraseology amounted to a permanent cessation even though that word would not be used. The words 'complete' and 'definitive' would signify permanence. On Wednesday, 31 August 1994, an IRA statement caused huge political and media shock waves with an announcement which began:

> Recognising the potential of the current situation and in order to enhance the democratic process and underlying our definitive commitment to its success, the leadership of the IRA have decided that as of midnight, August 31, there will be a complete cessation of military operations.

Further on, the statement laid out what amounted to a condition for the continuance of the cessation:

> A solution will only be found as a result of inclusive negotiations. Others, not least the British government, have a duty to face up to their responsibilities.

This was the sting in the tail. The main players, Reynolds, Hume, Adams and McGuinness, stated explicitly or strongly implied that the IRA cessation was permanent. To the activists down the line this was not so certain. They had debated an 'open-ended' cessation and were quickly told after the announcement that there would be a return to armed actions if things did not go as expected. Some of this was for internal cohesion to bring the doubters along. The reality was that the leadership intended the cessation to be *lasting*, provided the British faced up to 'their responsibilities' ie, delivered inclusive, unconditional negotiations on an open agenda.

This was a huge turn-around by the Adams–McGuinness leadership: an indefinite cessation without a commitment by Britain to withdraw. The central features of the long war strategy had been shredded. Neither was this a truce with agreed terms. It was risky territory. What's more, for the first time they had made themselves reliant on others, notably the Irish government and to a lesser extent Washington, to ensure the goods were delivered. It meant the Army Council and GHQ Staff took precautions to prevent the debilitating experience of the 1975 long truce, where British intelligence used the time and space to infiltrate and undermine the IRA organisation. This time the IRA decided to keep up a programme of training, intelligence-gathering and targetting. They also put in place a tightly controlled contingency plan, to target Britain if things went wrong. With that in mind a top secret engineering and bomb-making operation, already working at a remote house in Clonaslee, Co Laois, would become the hub of a resumed campaign in Britain.

OPTIMISM AND DISILLUSIONMENT, 1994–1995

At first, the IRA cessation created huge political momentum, wrong-footing the British government and the

Unionists, forcing the pace on a strong nationalist agenda. Though this was no agreed truce, the Republican movement leadership believed that Sinn Féin would be at a negotiating table within three months and that British Army units would be phased back off the streets within a month. Reynolds did not feel bound by a commitment to talks within three months but rather within about six months, that is, after the 'Framework Document' on new political structures was agreed and proposed jointly by both governments. Reynolds had reason to believe that the British Prime Minister, John Major, was serious about upcoming negotiations. Major confided to the Irish Prime Minister that he had officials working on the legislative and constitutional changes required, including changes in the Government of Ireland Act, and that he envisaged completion of that process by the autumn of 1997.

At first events moved rapidly. Within a week, as promised, Albert Reynolds invited Gerry Adams to Government Buildings. On Tuesday, 6 September 1994, Reynolds, Adams and Hume symbolically interlocked hands in a triple handshake and pledged in a statement that they were 'totally committed to democratic and peaceful methods' of resolving their political problems. In parallel, across the Atlantic, veteran IRA leader Joe Cahill was rounding up support for the cessation, having been granted a visa by a hugely reluctant President Clinton. The American support bases stayed on board or stayed neutral and watchful. On all fronts a split was avoided.

The next month, on 13 October 1994, the Combined Loyalist Military Comman (CLMC) announced a ceasefire, partly the result of intermediary shuttling by northern Presbyterian Minister, Rev Roy Magee. In making their announcement the CLMC declared the Union with Great

Britain to be 'safe'. Fifteen days later, on 28 October, Gerry Adams and Martin McGuinness led a Sinn Féin delegation into the Forum for Peace and Reconciliation in Dublin Castle established by Reynolds under the terms of the 'Joint Declaration'. The concordat between militant and constitutional Irish republicanism seemed complete and irrevocable (leaving aside the as yet unannounced Continuity Army Council and the Irish National Liberation Army). Not since before the Treaty of 1922 had anything like this been witnessed.

There were straws in this warm wind, however. The British remained sceptical of IRA intentions. They took until 21 October to agree to a 'working assumption' that the cessation was permanent. It would be almost four months before British soldiers were removed from street duty. In between, on 10 November, members of South Armagh IRA shot dead a postal worker, Frank Kerr, during a robbery in Newry. Although the IRA leadership disavowed the action, privately the British government began to raise the question of what to do about IRA arms.

Then, in late November, came an extraordinary political crisis in Dublin over the Irish Attorney General's handling of an extradition case involving a paedophile priest. It led to Albert Reynolds's resignation as Fianna Fáil leader and Taoiseach. After more extraordinary twists a new three-party coalition government emerged comprising Fine Gael, Labour and Democratic Left with John Bruton as Taoiseach. Given the highly personal nature of Reynolds's involvement in recent events this created uncertainty in IRA ranks.

It was not until 15 December that the first 'exploratory' talks opened between British officials and a Sinn Féin delegation, led by Martin McGuinness and Gerry Kelly. Finally on 22 February 1995, John Major and John Bruton launched 'A New Framework For Agreement' in Belfast. It seemed the process of negotiation was about to proceed at last. The Framework Document, as it was known, was designed as a joint British–Irish proposal, their joint vision of what was achievable and which they would jointly pursue. The Framework Document gave great encouragement to the Republican movement, laying out as it did the need for 'new arrangements and structures' within Northern Ireland combined with North–South institutions with executive, harmonising and consultative functions 'to promote agreement among the people of the island of Ireland' in the context of a new balanced constitutional settlement.

For nationalists the launch of the Framework Document was a high point of optimism. For Unionists it heralded a process of betrayal by the British government. So destabilising was it that, in time, the leader of the Ulster Unionist Party, James Molyneaux, prematurely resigned. From the outset the Unionists had sought the complete disarmament and disbandment of the IRA before they would enter negotiations involving Sinn Féin. Soon, during the exploratory talks with Sinn Féin, the British side began raising the question of decommissioning IRA arms in advance of talks. By May 1995 the British government had found a device to stall the Unionist retreat and, by extension, stall the move to inclusive negotiations. This device became known as the 'Washington Tests', having been made public in Washington by the Northern Secretary, Sir Patrick Mayhew. Sir Patrick explained that before Sinn Féin could enter substantive negotiations with the British government there would have to be 'substantial progress' in decommissioning IRA weapons. This would involve:

> '... a willingness in principle to disarm progressively; agreement on the methods and means of decommissioning; some actual decommissioning to act as a sign of good faith, to test the procedures for decommissioning, and to signal the start of a process.'

The IRA Army Council never budged from its position, taken at the time of the cessation, that no arms would be handed up – not a single round – prior to an agreed settlement. Conversely, this meant that the IRA *would* face full and verifiable decommissioning as part of an overall settlement. It would be the price for getting *up* from the negotiating table rather than for sitting *down* at it. In their terms a settlement must involve overall demilitarisation, including a withdrawal of British troops and the creation of an acceptable, unarmed police service. One way or another, the Army Council had determined that a General Army Convention held at the *end* of the process would finally decide the issue.

These positions led to a stand-off, a serious delaying of negotiations which, in turn, fuelled a long hot summer of street tension and Sinn Féin protests. In particular, during July 1995, a hiatus over the re-routing of Orange Order parades resulted in outward defiance at Drumcree, near Portadown. A huge confrontation between Orangemen and the RUC convinced many in the British establishment that they could not proceed at the pace, or even in the direction, encapsulated in the 'Joint Declaration' and Framework Document. Though only a few on the Irish nationalist side understood it, Drumcree 1995 was a turning point, or at least a re-assessment point, for the British government.

RETURN TO 'WAR', 1995-1997

By early autumn 1995 the IRA Army Council had decided to return to armed action unless visible and progressive political movement could be attained. This decision was conveyed to a caucus meeting of about forty-five IRA leaders and commanders at Fanad, Co Donegal near the end of October. The contingency plans for a British bombing campaign were put at the ready.

One significant event prevented the move at that juncture, the visit to Ireland by President Clinton at the end of November. Clinton's impending visit had forced a last-minute agreement between London and Dublin on a twin-track way forward, exploring the route to negotiations in parallel with the question of arms decommissioning. Out of this came an International Body, chaired by former US Senator George Mitchell, to examine the arms issue. Politically, Clinton's visit to Northern Ireland encouraged the Adams 'camp' and generally created noticeable goodwill on both sides of the divide. In this period, however, Gerry Adams was privately warning sources in Dublin that he was 'losing the argument' internally. An IRA resumption could have been expected at any stage.

As the new year turned, further pressure was applied when, on 6 January 1996, the Continuity Army Council revealed its existence. Claiming leadership of the Irish Republican Army and pledging allegiance to the thirty-two county Republic, the CAC said 'action will be taken in the future at an appropriate time'. A number of prior and later bombing missions in Monaghan, Enniskillen, Derry and Belfast gave credence to the claim. It was a destabilising shot across the bows and a red light warning for unhappy IRA activists.

Adams effectively lost the argument on 22 January 1996. That was the day the International Body published its report which amounted to a rejection of the British arms-before-talks Washington Test. Tactically, John Major buried his embarrassment and, disguising the fact that his government accepted the Mitchell Report, insisted that the route to negotiations would now be via an election to a Forum in Northern Ireland. It was then seventeen months after the IRA cessation and no fixed date for inclusive talks had yet been set.

On 9 February, the IRA announced the end of its cessation and almost simultaneously a huge bomb exploded in Canary Wharf, London. It killed two men, and caused massive destruction. In their statement the IRA did not show a reversion to a 'Brits out' policy but rather called again for an 'inclusive negotiated settlement'. The decision to end the cessation caused considerable upheavals within the Republican movement and their heartlands. Systems of communication which had been put in place during the cessation were ignored. Leading community activists who should have been forewarned were left in disarray. The final decision to go with the Canary Wharf bomb was made by a majority of the Army Council but not with all members present. Huge tension built up. Internally the decision was viewed by critics as a tactical success (it propelled political events forward) but a strategic disaster (it weakened the IRA's long-term negotiating position).

Further, the British government had, in effect, agreed a fixed date for talks and had communicated this to Washington prior to the bomb. The Irish Foreign Minister, Dick Spring, got news of this during talks at the White House. On 9 February, returning home by plane in better spirits, Spring's entourage heard about the Canary Wharf bomb.

Within a short time the two governments had agreed a fixed date for talks, 10 June 1996. In negotiations with London, Spring had gone way out on a limb, insisting on a role at the talks for George Mitchell. This would internationalise the negotiations in the person of President Clinton's close confidante and, as such, was a key demand of Sinn Féin. In agreeing a central role for Mitchell, John Major backed Dublin against the Unionists, casting aside the strenuous objections of the Unionist Party leader, David Trimble.

It was a significant and brave move by the British Prime Minister, given his government's ever-increasing reliance on Unionist votes at Westminster. Dublin had insisted, and London had complied, because Spring felt he had received assurances from Sinn Féin that this package would bring a positive IRA response. When the IRA failed to restore their cessation, Spring's people felt betrayed and told senior Sinn Féin figures as much in the midst of a flaming row.

There remained the prospect that the IRA would restore the cessation in time to allow Sinn Féin enter the talks on 10 June. During the preceding Forum election, Adams further fuelled this expectation. He stated that Sinn Féin would sign up to what was called the Mitchell principles, a set of six commitments to non-violence for participants at the talks. This enhanced Sinn Féin's standing at the polls and the party ended up with more than 115,000 votes, their highest since the 1950s.

When it came to the start of the talks there was no IRA cessation and, therefore, no place at the table for Sinn Féin. But division in the ranks of the Republican movement was made public when *An Phoblacht* published the speech Adams had prepared for the opening session at Castle Buildings in Stormont, Belfast. In the prepared speech, Adams described the talks as 'the historic opportunity ... a unique and unprecedented opportunity to forge a peace accord for all the people of the island.' There could be no clearer indication that Adams thought the time had come to start talking and stop bombing.

Almost simultaneously, on 15 June, a 1.5 ton IRA bomb exploded in Manchester City centre, causing huge destruction and injuring about 200 people. It came a week after an IRA unit shot dead a Garda, Gerry McCabe, during a post office raid in Adare, Co Limerick. On 20 June, Gardaí uncovered the IRA's top secret bomb-making 'factory' at Clonaslee, Co Laois, revealing deadly intent for action across the water. This, in turn, led to further arrests and huge home-made bomb discoveries in London, undermining almost the entire planned British campaign. Also in this period, some of the IRA's most senior engineers and previously unknown 'sleepers' were taken into custody. Yet the IRA remained extremely well equipped. Almost half of the Libyan haul of arms from a decade previously – 2,500 kilos of Semtex and 585 Kalashnikov rifles – was still in IRA hands. The armed option had not been discarded, especially with mounting tension in the north.

The summer of 1996 saw Drumcree Mark 2, an even more inflammatory repeat of the stand-off between Orange Order marchers and the police. This time Sinn Féin was prepared, with activists placed in resident and community groups ready to face down and block Orange marches through Catholic areas. Overall, these events strengthened the Republican movement's local bases of resistance, weakened the Unionists' image and undermined nationalist confidence in the RUC.

TOWARDS THE MILLENNIUM

As events moved on through 1996 fresh moves were in place to get a renewed IRA cessation. John Hume and Gerry Adams put together another initiative. They sought a guaranteed entrée for Sinn Féin into the Stormont talks in the event of an unequivocal restoration of the cessation; provided the talks were unconditional and time-framed. In the midst of Hume's shuttling diplomacy with the British Prime Minister, the IRA further undermined his efforts. On 6 October, they exploded two bombs within British Army HQ at Lisburn, Northern Ireland, on the eve of the Conservative Party Conference at Bournemouth. One soldier died from his injuries.

In IRA parlance these bombs were designed to show John Major that, while they wanted *in* to talks, they were not in the business of surrender. But the Lisburn bombs caused serious internal disturbance within the Republican movement and led, in early November, to a reconstituted IRA Executive and Army Council. The Army Council now had a new Chief-of-Staff, a veteran militant from South Armagh, and three senior Sinn Féin figures. The balance had tilted back again, probably five to two, in favour of the political path.

While the IRA resumed operations on a limited scale inside Northern Ireland, 1997 brought a degree of hope that politics would win the day. The Combined Loyalist Military Command had not ended their ceasefire, though some loyalist-oriented bomb attacks had followed IRA actions. The reconstituted Army Council had taken the decision to reinstate the cessation. That was the vital thing. The political strategy remained intact. It was a matter of timing and of ascertaining confidence in British intentions. Martin McGuinness said the IRA moved first on the previous occasion in August 1994, this time the British would have to move first.

The fact was the IRA leadership had put in place a system to monitor a renewed cessation. The new Executive would review the situation within four months and thereafter. The hardliners, seeking full-scale 'war' had been beaten back. The advocates of politics were in control. Yet the leadership had made it plain and public that they could revert to 'direct' action if inclusive negotiations were not available. In the end Sinn Féin would enter inclusive negotiations. They could expect the same policy under a new Labour Prime Minister in Downing Street, Tony Blair.

These were fraught times. The Republican movement's moral position had been seriously undermined by the resumed campaign. The Adams–McGuinness leadership was on trial, and potentially in jeopardy, like never before. The Army Council could still not guarantee success, either through politics or armed action. British withdrawal was not in prospect. They could no longer claim the 'powers of government' as justification for their existence. They *could* claim to have held the ground for their people and also that, uniquely since the 1920s, they had not been beaten. In the right circumstances they could look forward to real 'irreversible' change and a sense of equality for northern nationalists. Arguably that limited objective had always been attainable without armed force. This raised a very grave question: was the price worth paying? The Provisional IRA had killed about 1,800 people and inflicted so much hurt and destruction. All that was on offer after the long long war was a minority place at the negotiating table. One thing was certain. More than three-quarters of a century on from the 1916 Rising and the Treaty the Irish Republican Army, Provisional *and* Continuity, still felt it had a mission to complete, a mission which looked set to bring it into the new millennium.

POLITICS CONQUERS WAR, 1997–2000

If the IRA's mission was set to continue it was also destined for further division. The militarists within were determined never to give up the Holy Grail; for them it could only be undiluted 'Brits out'. In the end, they held fast and the IRA split again. But the Adams–McGuinness leadership kept the great majority on board as they jumped on the political train, which began an unstoppable journey into uncharted territory once Britain's new Prime Minister took the driver's wheel.

When Tony Blair came to office on 1 May 1997, with a massive House of Commons majority of 178 seats, he instantly wielded his power and authority on the Irish Question, challenging, in turn, the Republican Movement and the Ulster Unionists to face uncomfortable political compromises. By a strange symmetry, on 6 June that year power changed hands in Dublin, too. Fianna Fáil's leader and deal-maker, Bertie Ahern, became Taoiseach, in coalition with a junior partner, the Progressive Democrats. In Washington, US President Bill Clinton was still installed and still strongly engaged. These were powerful political centres, capable of bringing great pressure to bear when necessary.

Sinn Féin was also showing measurable results for its political strategy. Both Gerry Adams and Martin McGuinness had won (abstentionist) seats to Westminster in the recent British general election, on an overall increased Sinn Féin vote. The party made more history when Caoimhghín Ó Caoláin was elected to Dáil Éireann for the constituency of Cavan–Monaghan. He was the first Sinn Féin candidate elected to the Dublin parliament since the party dropped its policy of abstention eleven years previously and the first ever anti-treaty Sinn Féin member to take a seat there since the Civil War of 1921–1923. It was a measure of the Republican Movement's dramatic shift to pragmatic politics and the setting aside of seemingly immutable principles. After all, in the IRA's Green Book and in Sinn Féin's constitutional doctrine Dáil Éireann was still described as an 'illegal puppet regime'.

All round, in Britain and Ireland, political change was tangible. Fresh impetus was injected into the faltering peace process. Crucially, Tony Blair and Bertie Ahern delivered on Adams's repeated demand for a 'dynamic' in the drawn-out negotiation process in Belfast, namely a cut-off point for all-party agreement. The immediate result was the restoration of the IRA's 'complete cessation of military operations', announced on 19 July 1997. Sinn Féin was promised a place at the negotiation table, provided the cessation held.

When Sinn Féin negotiators finally took their places in the all-party talks at Stormont Castle, Belfast, on 9 September 1997, they signed up to the Mitchell Principles of non-violence and set the scene for another bloody rift within the Republican Movement. Already, those on the outside, the Continuity IRA, had made their point, with a powerful bomb in Markethill, County Armagh, the day formal talks began at Stormont Castle. Inside the (Provisional) IRA, discontent gathered around three senior figures: the Director of Engineering in Dublin; the Quartermaster General in Louth; and the former long-time Chief-of-Staff in Monaghan. These three disaffected leaders and their close associates could muster thirty years' experience in bomb-making and guerrilla operations. Their problem was how to handle opposition to the Adams–McGuinness strategy, which was clearly leading to a 'sell-out' on the final aim of an all-Ireland Republic. There was little appetite for a split and virtually none for an alliance with the Continuity IRA. Still, in time a serious and significant effort was made to resume a sustained armed campaign by those people who considered themselves the 'Real IRA'.

It began in early October 1997 when a General Army Convention was held at Carrigart, County Donegal. This meeting was, in effect, a pre-emptive strike by the Adams–McGuinness leadership to stave off a simmering leadership challenge. By varying votes, the dissidents ended up split. All along, their game-plan had been to stay inside the Movement and gather support for a change of policy. In reality this would mean toppling the leadership. But, in a seemingly hasty move, the Quartermaster General resigned, after being removed from the IRA Executive at the Convention. Some key figures went with him. But his closest ally, the Director of Engineering, stayed in. An ensuing attempt to force a wave of resignations in support of the Quartermaster General failed, leaving the dissidents in some confusion. Still, the die was now cast.

A resumed armed campaign was inevitable, driven by a powerful combination of operatives inside and outside the Republican Movement. The key question for internal dissidents seeking 'action' was: could a resumed campaign be *sustained*. If so, it would undoubtedly draw recruits. If not, it would be dismissed as 'stunting' – reduced to one-off bombing 'stunts' – as the Continuity IRA was dubbed. From early 1998 the Real IRA was gearing up, preparing to replicate the complete Provisional IRA structure of Army

Executive, Army Council, GHQ Staff, commanders, the lot. Potential recruits could be pointed towards the fraught Stormont Castle talks for evidence of ensuing treachery.

It was becoming increasingly clear that the deal on offer at Stormont would be hugely uncomfortable for the IRA and Sinn Féin. Taoiseach Bertie Ahern and Ulster Unionist leader David Trimble were forming a strong axis. Dublin and London were also setting out a joint stall. To the dismay of many in Sinn Féin, what was emerging was a new Northern Ireland administration, stronger than the North–South elements in any agreement. The complete reverse of what the Republican Movement sought, this would have the unmistakable appearance of a 'partition-ist' settlement, copperfastening British rule in a more modern form. Adams tried, but failed to get Ahern to move away from this formula. For his part, Trimble would have to swallow very hard on a major prisoner release programme, which was regarded as a vital 'selling' element for the paramilitary organisations on both sides. Prisoner release was not what the IRA had fought for; nor for equality within Northern Ireland. What they *had* fought for – Brits out – was being left for another generation, if at all. The dissidents felt certain that their day was coming. During February 1998, Real IRA operatives joined with others to mount two major bombing attacks, one on an RUC station in Moira, County Down, and the other, a bigger one, on Portadown's commercial centre. Significant movements of skilled home-made bombs on their way to targets were intercepted by the security forces north and south. In parallel, a thinly disguised political ally, the 32-County Sovereignty Committee, was touring the land for recruits and support. The Real IRA's structure and capabilities were building up.

Then came the political agreement, finally signed on Good Friday, 10 April 1998, following agonising last-ditch brinkmanship by Sinn Féin and the Ulster Unionists. By any reckoning, 'sell-out' or not, the Good Friday Agreement represented a huge advance for northern nationalists, the biggest since the failed Sunningdale Agreement of 1973 and, if it endured, the most significant since Ireland was partitioned in 1920–1921. It gave nationalists, the SDLP and Sinn Féin guaranteed ministries in a new Northern Ireland Executive Government, according to their party strengths, and set in motion structured North–South ministerial co-operation on an all-island basis. A British–Irish Council would informally link administrations in Dublin, Belfast, London, Edinburgh and Cardiff, as well as the Isle of Man and the Channel Islands. A Commission on Policing promised major police reform, tilting the balance evenly between both communities. All 'political' prisoners would be released within two years. Most contentiously, as it happened, participants to the Agreement were committed to the 'total disarmament of all paramilitary organisations' to be carried out through an independent Commission, headed up by General John de Chastelain. Both Governments would remove their respective 'claims' on Northern Ireland, leaving the constitutional future in the hands of its people.

To underwrite this truly historic accommodation, separate referendums would be held in both jurisdictions, North and South. For Sinn Féin and the IRA to accept this package was to shift hugely from their mission goal of 82 years' duration, established in the Proclamation of 1916: a 32-County Irish Republic to be decided upon by the Irish people acting as a single unit. Yet this shift was made, by the IRA acquiescing in, and then combining with a special

Sinn Féin Ard Fheis (conference) in Dublin on 10 May 1998. The required two-thirds majority for participation in the new Northern Assembly/Administration was easily achieved when 331 of the 350 voting delegates raised their hands in its favour. Inside, the Adams–McGuinness leadership was triumphant. Outside, their armed opponents were preparing to strike – hard.

The IRA's political and armed strategists were beginning a dance to the death, each trying to outflank the other. Most victories went to the political side. On 22 May both referendums were carried, by a big majority (71 percent) in Northern Ireland and by a steamroller majority (94.5 percent) in the Republic. Then on 24 June 1998, the day before elections to the new Assembly in Belfast, the Real IRA detonated a huge car bomb deep in Provisional IRA territory: Newtownhamilton, County Armagh. But when it came to the Assembly election results, Sinn Féin had marked up its biggest percentage since the peace process began, 17.65 percent, and entitlement to two out of twelve ministries in the Executive Government. On 1 August, with the new Assembly up and running, a Real IRA car bomb devastated the heart of Banbridge, County Down. Dissidents were growing in confidence and number. Then the Real IRA dealt themselves an almost fatal blow when, on 15 August, their bomb killed 29 people and injured about 250 in Omagh, County Tyrone. The subsequent outrage was such that the Real IRA, now in retreat and collapsing, called a ceasefire. But they continued styling themselves Óglaigh na hÉireann, The IRA, keeping alive their mission and their threat.

The political game was now well and truly the only one to play. Gerry Adams, Martin McGuinness, Pat Doherty and Martin Ferris, its leaders, were vindicated, if still with battles to fight.

By the autumn of 1998, the full implementation process contained in the Good Friday Agreement had stalled. David Trimble and his party were holding out for a start to IRA arms decommissioning before they would accede to fully establish the new Executive Government. Impasse turned to deadlock over this issue, even after US President Bill Clinton came to Ireland on 3 and 4 September and after Tony Blair became the first British Prime Minister to address the Dáil on 26 November 1998, each showing support and exerting pressure.

As events turned into the last year of the twentieth century, the glowing optimism of the year before slowly gave way to foreboding as the Republican Movement and the Ulster Unionists stole centre-stage in a stony face-to-face confrontation. No guns, no Government, was Trimble's cry. No Government, no guns, replied Sinn Féin. The first anniversary of the Good Friday Agreement came and went and still no agreement on the Executive and decommissioning. All this time the IRA and Sinn Féin insisted that decommissioning was 'voluntary', leaving many to believe that it might never happen at all. If it *did* happen, this would be the first generation of IRA leaders to 'surrender' arms, however voluntary and whatever the political gains for northern nationalists. Yet there it was in the Good Friday Agreement: the total disarmament of all paramilitary organisations. Would-be dissidents, particularly Real IRA activists who were now being recharged with hope, watched for this final 'betrayal'. Such an historic move on arms did seem to be on offer when Tony Blair and Bertie Ahern went to Belfast to broker a deal at the end of June 1999. Blair talked enthusiastically of 'seismic shifts' when Sinn Féin produced a proposal strongly suggesting a timetable for IRA decommissioning, once the Executive Government was guaranteed. Yet Blair's so-called 'absolute deadline' for a deal passed too.

By September 1999 it seemed the whole Good Friday Agreement was in freefall, even though more than 200 IRA prisoners had already been released and the Commission on Policing had recommended radical, sweeping changes to police structures, symbols and religious balance. Once again the Adams–McGuinness leadership was facing instability. But, in reality, the peace process was more robust than many feared. The ever-swinging pendulum of hope and fear was to move again, quite decisively, towards hope. Senator George Mitchell had been invited to re-enter the fray and conduct a Review. His remit was to find agreement between the parties on arms decommissioning and formation of the Executive Government. Eventually, through interminable twists during three months of talks, he did. On Tuesday, 16 November both Gerry Adams and David Trimble issued keynote statements, the fruits of their tortuous negotiations. Both expressed 'deep regret' for the suffering caused by the conflict. Trimble committed his party to supporting the Executive Government, once the IRA agreed to deal with the decommissioning body. On behalf of his party, Adams expressed total opposition to force for any political purpose.

Given the road Sinn Féin had travelled since its inception in 1905 and its interlocking involvement with the IRA's armed struggle from 1970 to 1997, this was groundbreaking stuff. Furthermore, Adams accepted that arms decommissioning was an 'essential' part of the peace process. Who would have thought it – the IRA's irredentist Green Book ideology in shreds!

Page by page, history was being made. On 2 December, at the Stormont Parliament in Belfast, the new Executive

Government for Northern Ireland was formed. Martin McGuinness, former IRA chief, was now Minister for Education. Sinn Féin's other ministry, Health, went to Bairbre de Bruin. The Ulster Unionists and the SDLP each had four ministries and Ian Paisley's Democratic Unionist Party, two. David Trimble, Unionist, and Seamus Mallon, nationalist, were First Minister and Deputy First Minister. John Hume, the principal architect of much of this new political structure, stood aside from office, partly for health reasons, as did Gerry Adams. That same day, in line with the Mitchell Review deal, the IRA announced that it was appointing a representative to discuss arms decommissioning with General John de Chastelain's Commission. Historians will mark 2 December 1999 as a truly significant date.

Eleven days later, on 13 December, in Armagh City, the first full meeting of the North–South Ministerial Council took place. Facing each other across a table were the entire Irish Cabinet and ten of the twelve new Northern Ireland ministers, there in good faith to begin an historic journey. (The two Democratic Unionist Party ministers stayed away in protest at Sinn Féin's involvement.) Not since Partition had nationalist and Unionist Ireland met in this fashion, to forge a co-operative future. That same week, on 17 December 1999, the British–Irish Council gathered in London, both islands healing the residues of their unhappy history.

Then, just as a bright new future began taking shape, that unhappy history paid yet another visit to the present. The issue, again, was IRA arms. It had become clear that the IRA's first engagement with the de Chastelain body was positive. Real movement on actual arms decommissioning seemed to be just around the corner, in line with the agreed sequence of events which emerged from the Mitchell Review. David Trimble had made it plain that his expectation was for a start on IRA decommissioning before the end of January 2000. But, as the end of that fateful month loomed, a crisis beckoned. General de Chastelain's second report, delivered past midnight on the night of 31 January, showed a stalling on the part of the IRA. Claiming default on the part of the Republican Movement, David Trimble called on the British Government to suspend the new institutions or face a pullout by him and his fellow ministers. In swift succession the Secretary of State for Northern Ireland, Peter Mandelson, began legislative moves to suspend the new Executive Government and Assembly in Belfast and to reintroduce Direct Rule from Westminster. Amidst frantic efforts by the Irish Government to get a further move from the IRA, the brink was reached.

At 5pm on Friday, 11 February 2000, Peter Mandelson signed the Direct Rule Commencement Order. Then, an hour and a half later, at 6.30pm, General de Chastelain issued a further report to the two Governments which added greatly to the unfolding drama. The General's report signalled a potentially momentous IRA move, enough for de Chastelain to conclude that a real prospect then existed for his Independent International Commission on Decommissioning to 'fulfil its mandate', ie, achieve full arms decommissioning. Of course, as always, it wasn't that simple. The IRA had still to make a definitive commitment to actual decommissioning. But they had told the de Chastelain body that they would 'initiate a comprehensive process to put arms beyond use'. They would 'consider' doing this in the context of other aspects of the Good Friday Agreement being implemented, in particular British demilitarisation and reform of the police and the judicial system. This implied a long drawn-out process, perhaps lasting years, going far beyond the aspirational deadline of May 2000 contained in the Good Friday Agreement for complete arms decommissioning. Yet, just as dramatically as they had made their tantalising move, the IRA pulled back.

Five days later, on 16 February, the IRA leadership withdrew from the de Chastelain body, taking all existing offers off the table when it became clear that the British Government would not immediately reinstate the new political institutions. It was all too frantic and unfinished for the British Government. Prime Minister Tony Blair feared an uncontrolled unravelling of the peace process if David Trimble was forced to reconsider his resignation threat in these uncertain circumstances. So everything went on hold as yet another search got underway to 'move the process forward', as the tired cliché of the day had it.

Still, the fundamentals remained in place. Gerry Adams and David Trimble stayed publicly and privately committed to the Good Friday Agreement. The IRA made it plain that their 'complete cessation' would hold. All parties held their breath and held their nerve, ready to continue this extraordinary journey. Despite all of its compromises, especially its 'partitionist' shape, the Good Friday Agreement was still regarded by the IRA as a vehicle for achieving a lasting peace. Yet, as they themselves knew, none of this guaranteed a united Ireland or 'Brits out'. In the stretch of history, this represented an astounding new pragmatism.

More likely, the endgame would be more complex than a simple united Ireland solution. The Good Friday Agreement laid out a wider framework for the future. Those new interlocking relationships on the island of Ireland and between Britain and Ireland would be the pattern for foreseeable generations. An expanding European Union would give it all fresh focus too, encouraging future generations to look outwards for their political identity, rather than inwards to narrow, ancient battlefields.

In the period ahead there would still be crises and torment, especially over IRA arms and British demilitarisation. The Real IRA was expected to regroup and strike again, this time in Britain. The Continuity IRA was calling on the Provisionals to hand over to them the weapons that were 'procured to defend the Republic' as established in 1919. But the general belief had grown that the Irish people would not give much succour to killing for Ireland in the name of a dying ideology. It would be some years yet before that hopeful presumption could be tested to the full.

ARMS BEYOND USE, 2000–2003

If the test for an end to physical-force Irish republicanism was an end to the current 'Provisional' IRA armed struggle, then events might suggest that the Provisionals had passed that test. In June 2000, the IRA had opened some of its arms dumps for independent inspection. In October 2001 and April 2002, they put significant amounts of arms 'beyond use', as the new phraseology had it – happenings variously described by IRA leaders as 'historic' and 'unprecedented'. By early 2003, the IRA was holding out the prospect of 'definitively' setting aside its arms by decision of an IRA General Army Convention. *Closure* and *completion* were the buzz words. These events, however, did not constitute the full picture.

IRA moves on arms came amidst continuing crises in the Irish peace process. Suspicion about the IRA's actions and long-term intentions continued to destabilise the political institutions of the Good Friday Agreement. In the wings, the Continuity IRA made it plain and very public that they and Republican Sinn Féin considered themselves the core of the legitimate Republican movement. There would be no ceasefire from that quarter. At the same time, the Real IRA remained externally active but internally turbulent.

The great majority of operatives, that is those within the Provisionals, remained on cessation of violence. A firm belief had grown among them that their armed struggle was permanently over, although it was not firmly announced in those terms. There remained the struggle over the context for final closure. For many, this had to be an 'irreversible thrust' towards Irish re-unification not simply the implementation of the Good Friday Agreement. That was what the volunteers had been promised from the start and many would watch the complicated political manoeuvrings of Gerry Adams for any signs of departure from this. Within the other IRA groupings, a good number of experienced activists – upwards of a hundred – were determined to continue the armed fight for the Republic. Whether silent and beyond use or active and at the ready, the gun was set to remain a force in Irish republican politics.

BREAKING THE LOGJAM

With the political institutions suspended from February 2000, the search was on for a solution to break yet another logjam. How could the new Northern Ireland Executive and Assembly be got up and running again? How could the IRA be engaged in the promised 'comprehensive process to put arms beyond use'? The crisis seemed especially grave. It had taken an inordinate time and effort to find a way of getting Ulster Unionist leader David Trimble to enter the power-sharing Executive involving Sinn Féin. IRA and Sinn Féin strategists were wrong-footed by the suspension of the institutions, expecting that neither government would want to dismantle these, having exhausted such political capital in getting them going. Stalemate ensued.

In Washington the following month, President Clinton's door to Sinn Féin leaders was less than fully open. It was the time of the St Patrick's Day celebrations and, more than any other US President, Bill Clinton had extended exceptional access to all participants in the Irish peace process. The previous October/November, Clinton had again 'given' Senator George Mitchell to Ireland, and there was a feeling in the White House that the Irish Republican movement had effectively reneged on the deal done with Mitchell. By agreeing to meet the Independent International Commission on Decommissioning in December 1999, it was assumed that the IRA would deliver *actual* decommissioning. During the final stages of the Mitchell Review, David Trimble had made it clear to Gerry Adams, George Mitchell and both governments that he would not remain in the Executive longer than two months if the IRA had not delivered.

The IRA rejected charges of betrayal on its part. 'The IRA has never entered into any agreement, undertaking or understanding at any time with anyone on any aspect of decommissioning,' the IRA had said in a public statement that was received with astonishment all round. This statement, made on 5 February 2000, came two months after the IRA's representative formally engaged with the

Independent International Commission on Decommissioning. 'We have not broken any commitments or betrayed anyone,' the statement asserted. This seemed to defy logic and the politics of the situation. The Mitchell Review had had a strictly two-item agenda: how to get the Executive formed and decommissioning started.

In concluding his review, George Mitchell had said: 'I believe that a basis now exists ... for the institutions to be established and for decommissioning to take place as soon as possible'. Mitchell is believed to have reported to US Secretary of State Madelaine Albright and President Clinton that the IRA would begin decommissioning by the end of January 2000. It was their failure to do this that caused the breakdown and resulted in the Commission's pessimistic suggestion that it be disbanded if decommissioning was not to happen. Still, what the IRA *had* promised within days of that gloomy assessment, and under extreme pressure from the Irish Government, was a qualified promise to initiate a process of putting its arms beyond use within a somewhat ambiguous 'context'. That was not enough to solve the political implosion. In the long run, however, it was a huge move, albeit one enveloped in a smokescreen of wordplay. Unfolding events would show that the IRA had now accepted the *principle* of engaging in a legalised process of decommissioning.

IRA STRATEGIES

Internally, IRA volunteers understood that their leadership would make a move on the arms issue by May 2000. This would be done by extracting more from the British Government, not just the re-establishment of the Executive but on a broad agenda that included in particular policing reform and British demilitarisation. Specifically, the IRA and Sinn Féin leaderships were bargaining, firstly to extend the time for decommissioning well beyond the two-year deadline enshrined in the Agreement, and secondly to get the legal terms for decommissioning changed to match their concept of a truly voluntary act. They sought to prevent decommissioning from becoming a 'white flag' issue – that is, an act of surrender. In their own eyes they were an undefeated army and they would strive to ensure that their armed struggle did not become criminalized or de-legitimised. After all, volunteers had been 'Green--Booked' in the notion that the IRA Army Council was the 'Lawful Government of the Irish Republic', and all of them were members of a 'legal and lawful army'.

Now they were in the complicated and messy business of a peace process. Timing was of the essence. Bringing along the doubters was essential. Holding to their long-term objectives was crucial. From 2000 onwards, the IRA leadership was slowly and inexorably setting out in public the stall which its strategists had privately constructed some years back: a) the IRA *would* decommission arms but in the context of all-round disarmament involving the British forces; b) they would do so under their own control and Standing Orders with independent verification; c) their time-scale would be in the context of a final end to the conflict – in IRA terms, final British withdrawal from Ireland. Pursuing these objectives, the IRA would continue to insist that they were not party to the Good Friday Agreement and, therefore, not bound by its commitments. Naturally, neither government subscribed to these strategies or this line of thinking. In time, these differences would lead to a major confrontation between the IRA and the two governments. For the moment, however, ambiguity was tolerated in the interests of getting movement on all fronts.

COMPLETE AND VERIFIABLE AMBIGUITY

Ambiguity was manifest when a new accommodation was reached between both governments and all the parties in May 2000. On 5 May, the governments announced a joint programme of action to implement fully the remaining aspects of the Good Friday Agreement, by June 2001. David Trimble would seek to lead his party back into the Executive and the IRA would move significantly on arms decommissioning. The following day, 6 May, the IRA released a keynote statement that would become the touchstone document on its intentions about arms. 'The IRA will initiate a process that will completely and verifiably put IRA arms beyond use.' That was the headline, the breakthrough, that became the focus of much political and public attention. The statement went on to say that the IRA would resume contact with the decommissioning body 'on the basis of the IRA leadership's commitment to resolving the issue of arms'. The assumption was widely made that the IRA would conclude the process of decommissioning within a year, all other things being delivered.

That, of course, was not in line with the IRA's long-term strategy. Crafted ambiguities within the statement held their position intact. It was a carefully constructed and detailed exposition of their position on arms, far more complex than the headline-grabbing line. Nine paragraphs long, the statement in its second paragraph said:

> 'Republicans believe that the British Government claim to a part of Ireland, its denial of national self-determination to the people of the island of Ireland, the partition of our country and the mainte-nance of social and economic equality in the Six Counties are *the root causes of conflict*. [author's emphasis]'

This was matched by the fourth, key, paragraph:

> 'The full implementation, on a progressive and irreversible basis, by the two governments, especially the British Government, of what they have agreed will provide a political context, in an enduring political process, with *the potential to remove the causes of conflict* [author's emphasis] and in which Irish republicans, and unionists can, as equals, pursue our respective political objectives politically.'

Then it went on:

> 'In that new context the IRA leadership will initiate a process that will completely and verifiably put IRA arms beyond use.'

It was possible for all parties, including Unionists to read those ambiguous words to their own satisfaction. Early and complete decommissioning was expected. To IRA volunteers, 'removing the causes of conflict' meant nothing less than removing British jurisdiction from Ireland. Completion of the arms issue was a long way off. The IRA leadership had signed up only to initiate a process with no defined start or end date. Still, the ambiguity was sufficient. The suspension of the Northern Ireland Assembly and Executive was lifted from midnight on Monday, 29 May 2000. Sinn Féin Ministers Martin McGuinness and Bairbre de Bruin were back in government with David Trimble and other Unionists and nationalists. The IRA, on the outside, held fast to its long-term strategy. The pattern of advancing crisis by crisis would continue.

In making this latest advance, the IRA had clearly signalled their non-violent intentions. They were holding on to their weapons and command structure but were also digging in for the long political haul. Further, they had now agreed to independent inspections of arms dumps. That task would be carried out by two international figures – former President of Finland, Martti Ahtisaari, and former General Secretary of the African National Congress, Cyril

Ramaphosa, reporting regularly to the de Chastelain decommissioning body. The month of May 2000 was another milestone on the IRA's tortuous journey.

NO ACTUAL DECOMMISSIONING

While the IRA and Sinn Féin leaderships would attempt to control the route-map, the two governments and other parties had different plans and timetables. International events would also force the IRA's hand. For a start, Ulster Unionism was in a state of almost perpetual dissent over David Trimble's leadership and trust, or lack of it, in Sinn Féin and the IRA. Two reports by the arms inspectors, on 26 June and 26 October 2000, said that substantial amounts of explosives, related equipment, weapons and other material had been inspected and confirmed as secure. Still, no actual decommissioning had occurred, nor had agreement on the methods of doing so even been reached. As a result, David Trimble's party voted to prevent Sinn Féin ministers from attending North–South ministerial meetings. Another crisis, another impasse beckoned up the road.

Sinn Féin and the IRA were holding back in order to extract more on British demilitarisation and policing reform. Other nationalist groupings, including the Irish Government and the SDLP, also sought significant changes to the policing legislation, especially as it related to the independence of scrutinising bodies such as the Ombudsman. Neither the SDLP nor Sinn Féin had yet agreed to take their designated places on the proposed new Policing Board for the new Police Service of Northern Ireland. As for demilitarisation – or normalisation as the Agreement had it – during 2000, British Army troop levels, at under 13,500 soldiers, were at their lowest since 1970. At the full state of normality, troop levels could be down to 5,000. Moves to normality depended on the level of threat posed by paramilitary groups. In making their threat assessment, the British Army calculated paramilitary 'intent' and 'capability'. IRA intent was low: their cessation held firm. But as long as they remained intact and fully armed IRA, capability was high – possibly even higher than previously, given that they had a number of years to revise their procedures. That was the security assessment that kept troop levels relatively high and military watchtowers active in border areas like south Armagh. This in turn fed back into IRA attitudes to arms decommissioning.

Even by the third report of the arms inspectors, on 30 May 2001, where they re-inspected the same dumps, the IRA had still not put any weapons or explosives 'completely and verifiably beyond use'. More was to be extracted and more was. In all of this, the IRA and Sinn Féin were conscious of the outer limits of this brinkmanship. This yielded results but it also undermined the much-valued 'nationalist consensus', in particular the alliance of the Irish Government. Although Sinn Féin's electoral mandate had substantially grown and was expanded further in the Westminster General Election of 7 June 2001, the party was still not strong enough on its own. Martin McGuinness and Gerry Adams held their seats with increased majorities in the June election, and two more, abstentionist, MPs were added: Pat Doherty in West Tyrone and Michelle Gildernew in Fermanagh/South Tyrone. While Sinn Féin was still not strong enough to go it alone, it soon appeared that the IRA was capitalising on Sinn Féin's increased strength by pulling back even further on arms decommissioning. David Trimble was again threatening to pull out of the Executive. This time the Irish Prime Minister, Taoiseach Bertie Ahern, publicly demanded more from the IRA. Ahern felt let down, even betrayed, that the IRA had not delivered on its promise of May 2000. Mere inspections, he said, were not enough, neither were vague timetables.

THE WESTON PARK DEAL

By July, Trimble had resigned as First Minister of the Assembly and, again, the institutions were suspended. On 14 July 2001, at Weston Park in England, a crisis meeting of governments and parties again thrashed through the crisis issues: decommissioning, policing, normalisation/demilitarisation and the stability of the political institutions. A list of action points on these issues was announced by the governments, much of it contingent on IRA action. Deadlines for delivery were pushed back into late 2002. For the IRA, it represented another escape from the Good Friday time-scale, another advance on the arms issue.

The Weston Park agreement yielded key promises from the British Government: new legislation 'to reflect more fully' the Patten Report on policing to be enacted some time after October 2002; a progressive rolling programme reducing troop levels and army installations in Northern Ireland provided that there was 'a significant reduction in the level of threat' – that is, IRA arms decommissioning and closure on its activities.

This package of measures also marked a significant and notable change in the rules governing decommissioning. No longer would there be any implication of giving up or surrendering arms. To fit with the IRA's declared objective of putting its arms 'beyond use', the British and Irish governments passed new laws during August 2001. This legislation provided for a certified scheme whereby arms would be made 'permanently inaccessible or permanently unusable so that they are completely beyond use'. Locations would be agreed between the paramilitary contact person and the Independent International Commission on Decommissioning. The contact person could be the one to make a record of the arms put beyond use and the record would be verified by the Commission. These procedures fitted snugly with the IRA's concept of 'no white flag, no surrender'. This was formal recognition that the IRA had moved the goalposts. The scheme had been changed and the time-scale extended. The deadline for total disarmament laid down in the Good Friday Agreement was 22 May 2000. That had already been put back to June 2001. The new decommissioning scheme would end on 26 February 2002. In time, this too would be extended.

NINE-ELEVEN TURNS THE TIDE

Just as the IRA and Sinn Féin were gaining ground and re-gaining control of their own agenda, events far beyond their control interceded with traumatic effect. The date was 11 September 2001; the event: massive carnage at New York's international trade centre and the Pentagon in Washington when suicide bombers flew hijacked passenger-carrying aeroplanes into the buildings; the cause: Islamic grievances against US foreign policy. Suddenly 'terrorism' was so far beyond the pale that the new US President, George W. Bush, threatened to re-list the IRA as a terrorist group in a new 'war against terrorism'. The Real IRA and Continuity IRA were listed, precluding them from entering and fund-raising in the United States. Such a move against Gerry Adams, Martin McGuinness et al would constitute an enormously damaging retreat from gains already made. New York and Washington were not only vital places for the Sinn Féin political project but also important sources of finance for the party.

In addition, the arrest the previous month in Colombia of three 'republicans', suspected of training left-wing FARC guerrillas, came suddenly into very high relief. Some small arms trading in Florida had also come to notice. Tolerance for IRA ambiguities was zero. At this stage, in Northern Ireland, David Trimble was still resisting a return to the Executive with Sinn Féin because the IRA had failed to deliver product. Swiftly, Gerry Adams, ever the pragmatist, got on board with the US administration and Irish-American leaders.

On 23 October 2001, the decommissioning body reported the IRA's first act: a quantity of weapons, ammunition and explosives put completely beyond use. The Commission did not report the fact that some of the material had been under the control of south Armagh IRA, stored deep in the Republic. Internally, this carried special significance. South Armagh was a hard-line area where the IRA's chief of staff lived. In reality, the IRA had gone no further than a one-off act. They were not committed to a timetabled process of putting all arms beyond use and certainly not to a final date. Still, this on–off peace process was on again. Northern Ireland's political institutions were re-established. In an historic move, the other Irish nationalist party, the SDLP, decided to take its seats on the new Policing Board. For the first time since Ireland was partitioned in 1920–21, a large section of northern nationalists gave full allegiance to the local police service.

Sinn Féin was still refusing to endorse the Police Service of Northern Ireland or join the Policing Board despite entreaties to do so by Bertie Ahern, in Dublin. For the IRA and Sinn Féin, finality on arms and policing were two sides of the one coin. The strategies that they had worked out told them that this was not the time for completion on either arms or policing. As with the issue of IRA arms, the Republican movement placed policing within their long-term strategy. The ultimate litmus test was the prospect or otherwise of the development over time of an all-island policing structure. Within IRA ranks, 'finality' and 'completion' carried meanings far beyond the limits of the Good Friday Agreement.

ACTS OF COMPLETION

Yet those *were* the limits understood by all other parties to the Agreement. Finality was soon to become a demand from the British and Irish governments. The year 2002 was set to be one of completion and crisis. It began as a period when the Irish peace process was being bedded down. The Northern Ireland Executive and all-island North–South bodies functioned with renewed normality. On 8 April, the new Police Act came into force with the promised amendments. That same day, the arms decommissioning body reported a substantial amount of IRA weapons, ammunition and explosives put beyond use. In June, Sinn Féin made gains in the Irish general election, adding four more members to their one-man contingent in Dáil Éireann, the Irish parliament. The peace train was moving. Then, in September, its wheels came off. Several Sinn Féin figures were arrested and charged with 'spying' in various official government offices at Stormont in Belfast. David Trimble and the Ulster Unionists were about to exit the Executive for the third time when, on 14 October 2002, the British Government suspended the institutions, again. This was turned into make or break time.

Four days later, British Prime Minister Tony Blair came to Belfast and delivered a down-to-basics keynote speech. The time for ambiguities and inch-by-inch advances was over, he said. The crunch is the crunch, he told a large mixed audience. The fork in the road has finally come. 'We cannot carry on with the IRA half in and half out of this process.' This was not another impasse, said Blair, but a fundamental choice of direction. Now was the moment for 'acts of completion'. In Dublin, the Taoiseach, Bertie Ahern, endorsed Blair's line. Both governments were demanding acts of completion.

Immediate and intensive rounds of negotiations ensued. Six months passed. Every party seemed signed up to the endgame. Both governments would conclude a Joint Declaration containing a programme of completion, finalising all outstanding aspects of the Good Friday Agreement. As events moved on into the spring of 2003, a deadline loomed large: elections to the Northern Ireland Assembly in May. Still there was no finality. For its part, the IRA was expected to deliver a statement that its war was over, permanently, and in all aspects. Only then could Sinn Féin be back in government. This was, indeed, crunch time for the IRA and Sinn Féin. Internally, there was significant opposition to acceptance of these outer limits as the fulfilment of their active campaign.

HISTORY LESSONS

All other IRA campaigns since the Treaty of 1921 had ended in either defeat or inducement into partitionist constitutional politics. The prime example was Fianna Fáil. 'Fianna Fáil, the Republican Party' was established under Eamon de Valera's leadership back in 1926, having broken from the IRA with the promise that politics would deliver the all-Ireland republic. Fianna Fáil was the primary governing party in the Republic of Ireland for seventy years yet failed to deliver on that primary promise. Now, in the latter stages of the same century, a new brand of IRA leaders, notably Gerry Adams and Martin McGuinness, had vowed that *their* struggle would not end the same way. *They* would not be

'Fianna Fáilised'. They would keep the armed struggle or the armed option in being until Britain withdrew.

By 2003, many of these arguments had become more legalistic than real. In practice, Sinn Féin's elected representatives sat in Dáil Éireann, the Irish parliament in Dublin. Some of those new parliamentarians had been IRA volunteers schooled in the assertion that the same Dáil Éireann was an *illegal assembly, willing tool of an occupying force*. Volunteers had been required to look upon the Garda Síochána (Irish police) as an 'illegal force ... whose main task was treasonable'. So much had changed. Yet formally and legalistically not much had, as Tony Blair and Bertie Ahern found when they strove to get the IRA leadership to wrap up its mission. Most members of the IRA leadership and many of its activists had travelled the long road through almost three decades of armed conflict. Just as the IRA Green Book had stressed the illegality of the Irish parliament and police, it had strongly emphasised the legality and superiority of what it called its own Army Authority. All orders issued by this authority were said to be the 'legal actions and lawful orders of the Government of the Irish Republic'. This was described as 'one of the most important mainstays of the Republican movement'. (*IRA Green Book* pp.5-6). In these terms, the only reason for the IRA's existence was to fight for the re-establishment of the 32-county Irish Republic as proclaimed in 1919.

It was one thing to engage in pragmatic politics and pragmatic alliances with the current Irish Government in Dublin or take seats in the Stormont Assembly in Belfast. Those moves were explained as practical methods of broadening Sinn Féin's base of support and building up their mandate in pursuit of the IRA's long-term goal. That goal had a constitutional and legal imperative. In the IRA's constitution, the first objective is given solemnly: 'to guard the honour and uphold the sovereignty and unity of the Republic of Ireland, primarily by force of arms'. All of this still stood. The army authority still stood. To engage in these proposed acts of completion would be something momentous, truly historic. IRA leaders and volunteers were being asked both to end their historic mission a very long way short of that constitutional objective and to dispense with the armed option, permanently.

CRUNCH TIME

When crunch time arrived in early 2003, the IRA was unwilling to do this. What was requested by both governments was a clear, formal, written, public statement. Internally, what IRA strategists came up with was convoluted and ambiguous phraseology, designed to make significant advances while keeping their own flame burning and their historic mission alive. Negotiations came to breaking point. In the midst of this, US President George W. Bush flew into Belfast on 8 April to do business with Tony Blair about the on-going US-led war on Iraq, which was declared as part of the 'war on terrorism.' Bush also held meetings in Hillsborough Castle on the Northern Ireland negotiations, urging the parties to cement the peace. In a joint statement, President Bush, Prime Minister Blair and Taoiseach Bertie Ahern referred to their 'shared' view that the break with paramilitarism 'in all its past forms' must be 'complete and irreversible'. In the following days, back-channel talks continued apace with increasing optimism.

Finally, on 13 April 2003, the proposed IRA statement was passed confidentially to the two governments by Gerry Adams and Martin McGuinness. Its contents stalled everything. Blair and Ahern swiftly re-grouped in Downing Street. The statement had been delivered as the IRA's own act of completion but was rejected as such by Dublin and London – positive and an advance on previous statements, yes, said the governments, an act of completion, no; it was deemed neither clear nor unambiguous. The statement again said that the IRA was not party to the Good Friday Agreement; it signalled that they had authorised a third act of putting arms beyond use and would engage in a process with the decommissioning body. No time-scale was mentioned. On the vital question of a definitive end to paramilitary activity, the IRA had this to say:

> 'We are resolved to see the complete and final closure of the conflict. The IRA leadership is determined to ensure that our activities, disciplines and strategies will be consistent with this.

Furthermore, the full and irreversible implementation of the agreement and other commitments will provide a context in which the IRA can proceed to definitively set aside arms to further our political objectives. When there is such a context this decision can be taken only by a general army convention representing all volunteers.'

Clearly, this proposed a different sequence of events from that sought by the two governments. The IRA were not offering acts of completion on arms *now* as part of an all-round deal. Rather they would consider definitively setting aside arms *after* the Good Friday Agreement had been irreversibly implemented. Only then would there be a context for decision by an IRA general army convention. This left the IRA in charge of the time-scale and interpretation of future events. London and Dublin sought clarifications on what all this really meant. Bertie Ahern asked if 'complete and final closure of the conflict' was in the context of the

Good Friday Agreement, fully implemented, or if it meant that a united Ireland was required. Tony Blair asked if the IRA was committing itself to put *all* arms beyond use and to end targeting, weapons procurement, punishment beatings and the other listed activities.

On 27 and 30 April, Gerry Adams publicly answered questions that had been raised but failed in the end to satisfy the governments or Ulster Unionists. Adams did appear to satisfy Dublin and London, if not David Trimble, on two points: 1) referring to the IRA statement, he said that it meant that all arms would be put beyond use; and 2) if the governments and parties fulfilled their commitments, this would provide the basis for the 'complete and final closure of the conflict'. When combined with the IRA statement, this became complex language and politics. It meant that the army authority would remain in being and in charge. The army authority would decide when to put all arms beyond use and when the conflict was over. By seeming to accept these assurances, Blair and Ahern showed that, despite their demands for absolute clarity, creative ambiguity remained in play. The point they stuck on was the specific list of paramilitary activities to be immediately and permanently ended. London and Dublin insisted that the IRA sign up to this list. The IRA refused. A last ditch attempt at final agreement was tried. Another deadline was extended.

Assembly elections were put back three weeks, to 29 May 2003, in the hope of achieving agreement. The Joint Declaration was specifically contingent on getting that agreement. For their part, Ulster Unionists were required to commit to the full and stable operation of the political institutions – no more withdrawing from the Executive or half-working the North-South Ministerial bodies. The IRA were specifically required to spell out in clear and unambiguous language an immediate, full and permanent cessation of all paramilitary activity, listed in the Declaration as:

> 'military attacks, training, targeting, intelligence gathering, acquisition or development of arms or explosives, other preparations for terrorist campaigns, punishment beatings and attacks and involvement in riots.'

The transition to exclusively democratic means must now be completed, it said. Effectively the new final deadline was April 2005, the date set in the Declaration for full demilitarisation and normalisation by the police and British Army. Normalisation was spelt out in detail: peacetime police patrols, closure of a wide range of named military installations, a permanent army garrison of just 5,000 troops, all of this dependent on the IRA making what was called an historic leap forward.

What was in prospect was the chance to move forward on an agreed progressive, comprehensive and purely political programme. As part of this, policing and judicial powers would be devolved from Westminster to the Northern Ireland Assembly within four years. This was radical and ground breaking. In addition, both governments agreed to bring closure to a controversial item on the IRA agenda, namely the untidy matter of 'on-the-runs' (essentially activists hiding abroad who had escaped from custody or who were wanted for specified scheduled offences committed prior to the signing of the Good Friday Agreement). London and Dublin would instigate legislation to permit these people to return to Ireland by way of a judicial process but without a realistic prospect of facing imprisonment. For the IRA's 'on-the-runs' this legalised 'amnesty' would constitute a very real act of completion.

SANCTIONS

There was one further bitter pill that the IRA and Sinn Féin would be required to swallow if they went with this deal: legal sanctions for misbehaviour. An Independent Monitoring Body would be established to ensure that paramilitary groups and British security forces, as well as political parties, complied with their undertakings. Findings from the four-person Monitoring Body, comprising two appointees by the British Government and one each by the Irish and US administrations, could result in serious sanctions against parties or individuals. These sanctions would come via votes in the Assembly, approving the Monitoring Body's findings, or legislation at Westminster. Sanctions would range from public censure to legal prosecution to exclusion from the political institutions. In practice, this held out the possibility of Sinn Féin's being excluded from the Northern Ireland Executive if the IRA failed to deliver on its commitments. Neither the IRA nor Sinn Féin endorsed the proposed monitoring system. It would lock them both together within the process like never before. Crucially, it would run counter to the IRA's strategy of staying outside, of not being party to the Good Friday Agreement. This way, Sinn Féin would be held directly accountable for actions authorised by the Army Council. The IRA and Sinn Féin weren't prepared to go that road. The governments, however, decided that what they called the 'deficit of mutual confidence between both communities' was such that assurance mechanisms of this kind were now necessary. London and Dublin made a formal agreement to proceed with the Independent Monitoring Body.

THE IRA SAYS NO

Taken together, these acts of completion would require a

monumental change of strategy by the leadership and volunteers of the Irish Republican Army. They were being asked to accept that, for them, the end of the road was the Good Friday Agreement. Winning the republic would be left to politics and luck. The 'arms of the republic' would be disposed of in the name of a partitionist agreement. This was to be the unambiguous price for Sinn Féin's continuance in government. For many it would be, not so much an act of completion, as an act of humiliation.

In the end, when it came down to bedrock, the IRA said *no*. Tony Blair took the decision, in the face of opposition from Bertie Ahern, to postpone the Assembly elections until the autumn. Yet another cut-off date for all party agreement became 15 November 2003. London and Dublin agreed that the next move was up to the IRA. After the breakdown, Bertie Ahern told the Irish Parliament that the alleged IRA activities that had brought down the Executive in October 2002 remained central to getting the new political institutions up and running again. Those political institutions were essential to Sinn Féin's project. Without them it would be hard to argue that politics could provide an alternative to armed struggle in pursuit of the republic.

AGENTS AND COLLUSION

As 2003 advanced, other factors played into the IRA mindset. Illegal and lethal collusion between sections of British Intelligence and RUC police Special Branch in murders by loyalist paramilitary groups was firmly established. Collusion was already known if not officially confirmed. Investigations by senior police officer Sir John Stevens into the murder, in 1989, of Catholic and Belfast solicitor Patrick Finucane concluded that his murder could have been prevented. Reporting in March 2003, Stevens referred to (

loyalist) agents being 'allowed to operate without effective control and to participate in terrorist crimes.' Nationalists, said Stevens, were known to be targeted but were not properly warned or protected by the police. Stevens' ongoing inquiries had already led to 144 arrests and 94 convictions. There was more to come. His findings caused deep unease among nationalists, underscoring Sinn Féin's reservations about the continuance of certain Special Branch officers in the new police service. Stevens bluntly referred to obstruction of his inquiries 'which was cultural in its nature and widespread within parts of the Army and RUC.' Crucial evidence was concealed from his team, he wrote. Then, just as the Republican movement was raising these issues as support for its hesitancy in arriving at acts of completion, fingers turned in its own direction.

In May 2003, simmering rumours about a British agent deep in IRA ranks burst into the public domain. Variously called 'steak knife' or 'stakeknife', the agent was said to be of very high rank in the IRA. He was allegedly outed by one of his former handlers in British Intelligence. So valuable was this agent that, in order to protect his identity, he had freedom to engage in or allow many murders and killing operations to proceed. This raised fundamental moral and political issues for the British Authorities. The Stevens inquiry team was looking to question 'stakeknife'. For the IRA, however, the revelations were potentially devastating if proven.

The agent was said to have operated for more than two decades. His rank within the IRA was such that he could have passed on information about names, operations, methods, equipment, explosives expertise and command structures from the top to the bottom of the organisation. He was said to be in a position to stymie virtually the whole thrust of the so-called Semtex war conducted from 1986 onwards which, in the end, failed to deliver the expected fatal blow to the British Government. This was a very grave allegation. Volunteers were asking big questions of the leadership. Do they believe 'stakeknife's' denials? Will they investigate the allegations? How come they were so compromised? After all, it was the failure of the 'Semtex war' which propelled the IRA leadership into concluding, around 1990, that the armed campaign had to end in favour of an uncertain and uncomfortable political compromise. The alternative had been to re-group and re-arm and continue the armed campaign for an unacceptable length of time. Now, when they were being asked to embrace highly uncomfortable acts of completion in pursuit of that political compromise, the 'stakeknife' talk cut a lesion in the heart of many a volunteer.

THE 'TRUE' REPUBLICANS

Meanwhile, others were piling on pressure, attempting to exploit the IRA's difficulties – people who claimed the mantle of 'true' militant Irish republicanism. The Real IRA continued to re-group and prepare as expected. But internal disagreement and various imprisonments split them into two groups and weakened their capability. Between the two groups they had an estimated 30 to 50 operatives with sufficient recent knowledge to acquire finance and armaments and make efficient bombs. Their strength lay along the Border. The Continuity IRA and Republican Sinn Féin were patiently building up their layers for the long haul. CIRA operatives numbered 30 to 40, organised in pockets north and south with strong groups in Fermanagh/Mid-Ulster and Limerick/Tipperary. The month of June 2002 had seen the public announcement of a new military command for Fianna Éireann, the traditional IRA youth section dating back to the 1920s. The Fianna pledged their allegiance to Republican Sinn Féin, the Continuity IRA and Cumann na mBan, the traditional women's paramilitary body. Another generation of Irish people was being called to the cause. At Easter 2003, a statement ensued from the Leadership of the Republican movement in which it was stated that Republican Sinn Féin was working for an alternative to the Good Friday Agreement, and the Continuity IRA was asserting the right of the Irish people to the ownership of Ireland. The Provisional IRA was being asked to disband and stand aside for the true Republican movement.

THE IRA IN RETREAT, 2003–2005

There was no standing aside by the IRA and that became a problem, even a crisis. The Provisionals, IRA and Sinn Féin, found themselves under enormous pressure. In time, they were forced to make the big moves – totally disarm and join the Police Service of Northern Ireland. This gave the Continuity IRA, Republican Sinn Féin, and other splintered groups, a certain edge. They wouldn't be deflected. For them the continued British presence was justification enough. Looking up ahead, more arms were sure to be procured for the Republic, however many were put beyond use for the Good Friday Agreement.

TENSION, DEFECTIONS and CHALLENGES

For now, from 2003 onwards, the Provisional IRA and the Adams political leadership found themselves facing mounting destabilising challenges. Already, defections from the Provisional IRA had led to significant 'fund--raising' losses. One leading defector, a so-called 'Director of Smuggling', took with him upwards of sixty operatives with the skills and networks for cross-border smuggling. Another group, from South Armagh, defected with specialist expertise in transporting explosives into Britain, of the kind that hit London's Canary Wharf with such devastating effect back in February 1996 when the IRA cessation was broken. On the other hand, upwards of 700 IRA prisoners had been released under the terms of the Good Friday Agreement. That relieved the IRA of a huge expense, the welfare of prisoners' families. This meant that a potential war chest was accumulating, even if the leadership had not formally designed it as such. Also, tensions existed within the IRA's seven-man Army Council as the price rose for a total end to the IRA's mission. The Chief-of-Staff, a farmer and key smuggler at the Louth-Armagh border, was being watched internally for signs that he might break off to 'fight for the Republic'. That would be calamitous for the political strategy.

Against that background renewed attempts were made to rekindle the stalled political deal, though not until politics delivered fresh strength to the Adams leadership. Two elections saw Sinn Féin make further gains. In November 2003 the postponed Northern Assembly election gave Sinn Féin the forward thrust they had long sought. They beat off the SDLP challenge and emerged as the largest nationalist party, poised to take the prestigious post of Deputy First Minister in a new Executive government for Northern Ireland. But, as always, life wasn't that simple. On the Unionist side the Rev. Ian Paisley's Democratic Unionist Party beat David Trimble's Ulster Unionist Party for Assembly seats. Now business would have to be done with Paisley. The price for the IRA would be higher still. That was for later. Sinn Féin's second triumph came in June 2004 when they won their first-ever seats in the European Parliament, one in Northern Ireland, taking John Hume's old seat – further humiliating the SDLP – and one in Dublin.

TALKS, PHOTOGRAPHS and FAILURE

Now the pieces were in place for renewed negotiations, again involving all Northern parties and the British and Irish governments. This time, IRA arms and activities were centre-stage. The IRA would have to commit to full and complete decommissioning plus a final end to all activities in advance, before Ian Paisley would come into the loop. Even then, Paisley's party wouldn't deal directly, face to face, with Sinn Féin until the IRA had actually disarmed. Protracted and entangled talks bore real fruit. Paisley and Adams were closing on a deal. By December 2004 a step-by-step sequence of events was in place, including one hundred per cent IRA arms decommissioning by year's end and permanent closure to all other paramilitary activity; a full commitment by Paisley's party to power-sharing with Sinn Féin and to working the North-South all-island bodies; devolving Policing and Justice powers from Westminster to the Northern Ireland Assembly and, by extension, Sinn Féin to engage fully with the Police Service of Northern Ireland. For the IRA and Sinn Féin this would be a final, fundamental crossing of the Rubicon.

It did not happen however, not then, not until another crisis had passed. In December 2004 the IRA said 'no' to complete decommissioning, claiming, perhaps with some justification, that Paisley was out to humiliate them by demanding 'repentance' plus photographic evidence of arms being decommissioned. But the IRA soon dealt their own, almost fatal, blow to a political deal.

The political shutters came down when the IRA was fingered a) for a massive £26.5 million robbery at the

Northern Bank in Belfast on 20 December 2004 and b) for knifing to death local man Robert McCartney in Short Strand East Belfast on 30 January 2005. Gerry Adams and Sinn Féin felt the full cascade of negative publicity, leading to a massive national and international condemnation of the IRA, and a shunning of Adams by the White House during the traditional St Patrick's Day festivities in March 2005.

END-GAME

These were the toughest of times for Sinn Féin. The pressure only relented when the IRA made the biggest move of all: ordering 'an end to the armed campaign' from 4.00pm on 28 July 2005 and later totally decommissioning its arsenal. The military project was finally finished. It was now down to politics alone. The next momentous step was taken, after more protracted political manoeuvrings. On 28 January 2007 a Sinn Féin party conference voted by over ninety per cent to accept the Police Service of Northern Ireland. It was end-game. On 7 March Sinn Féin made further seat gains in the Northern Ireland Assembly elections. Nineteen days later came a public concordat between Adams and Paisley. The new Northern Ireland power-sharing Executive with Paisley as First Minister and Martin McGuinness as Deputy First Minister started on 8 May. Sinn Féin had triumphed, but at a hefty price: accept Northern Ireland, no British withdrawal, no guaranteed United Ireland, no IRA. This was not how they all planned it thirty-eight years earlier when the Provisionals were born. Others had not stopped planning. The Continuity IRA, Real IRA and a new IRA group, styled Óglaigh na hÉireann, were reported to be active and dangerous. The military mission, much diminished and fractured, would be carried forward in the name of the Republic.